Workbook 15

Making Rational Decisions

Manage Information
Certificate
S/NVQ Level 4

Institute of Management Open Learning Programme

Series editor: Gareth Lewis
Author: Cathy Lake

the *Institute of Management*

FOUNDATION

Pergamon
Flexible
Learning

Pergamon Flexible Learning
An imprint of Butterworth-Heinemann
Linacre House, Jordan Hill, Oxford OX2 8DP
225 Wildwood Avenue, Woburn, MA 01801-2041
A division of Reed Educational and Professional Publishing Ltd

℞ A member of the Reed Elsevier plc group

OXFORD   AUCKLAND   BOSTON
JOHANNESBURG   MELBOURNE   NEW DELHI

First published 1997
Reprinted 1998, 1999

British Library Cataloguing in Publication Data
A catalogue record for this book is available from the British Library

ISBN 0 7506 3673 4

Typeset by Avocet Typeset, Brill, Aylesbury, Bucks
Printed and bound in Great Britain

FOR EVERY TITLE THAT WE PUBLISH, BUTTERWORTH-HEINEMANN
WILL PAY FOR BTCV TO PLANT AND CARE FOR A TREE.

Contents

Series overview

The Institute of Management Open Learning Programme is a series of workbooks prepared by the Institute of Management and Pergamon Open Learning for managers seeking to develop themselves.

Comprising seventeen open learning workbooks, the programme covers the best of modern management theory and practice, and each workbook provides a range of frameworks and techniques to improve your effectiveness as a manager, thus helping you acquire the knowledge and skill to make you fully competent in your role.

Each workbook is written by an experienced management writer and covers an important management topic or theme. The activities both reinforce learning and help to relate the generic ideas to your individual work context. While coverage of each topic is fully comprehensive, additional reading suggestions and reference sources are given for those who wish to study to a greater depth.

Designed to be practical, stimulating and challenging, the aim of the workbooks is to improve performance at work by benefiting you and your organization. This practical focus is at the heart of the competence based approach that has been adopted by the programme.

The structure of the programme

The design and overall structure of the programme has two main organizing principles, both of which are closely linked to the national standards for management developed by the MCI (Management Charter Initiative).

First, the workbooks are grouped according to the key roles of management.

- Underpinning the management standards are a series of **personal competences** which describe the personal skills required by all managers, which are essential to skill in all the main functional or key role areas.
- **Manage Activities** describes the principles of managing processes and activities, with service to the customer as an essential part of this.
- **Manage Resources** describes the acquisition, control and monitoring of financial and other resources.
- **Manage People** looks at the key skills involved in leadership, developing one's staff and managing their performance.

- **Manage Information** discusses the acquisition, storage and use of information for communication, problem solving and decision making.

In addition, there are three specialized key roles: **Manage Quality, Manage Projects** and **Manage Energy**. The workbooks cover the first two of these. Unlike the four primary key roles above, these are not compulsory for certificate, diploma or S/NVQ requirements, but provide options for the latter.

Together, these key roles provide a comprehensive description of the fundamental principles of management as it applies in any organization – commercial, maintained sector or not-for-profit.

Second, the programme is organized according to **levels of management**, seniority and responsibility.

Level 4 represents first line management. In accredited programmes this is equivalent to S/NVQ Level 4, Certificate in Management or CMS. Level 5 is equivalent to middle/senior management and is accredited at S/NVQ Level 5, Diploma in Management or DMS. There are two S/NVQs at Level 5: Operational Management and Strategic Management. The operations role is focussed internally within an organization on the maintenance of systems and standards of output, whilst the strategic role is focussed on the whole organization, including the external operating environment, and looks at setting directions.

Together, the workbooks cover all the background knowledge you need to have for all units of competence in the MCI standards at Level 4 and Level 5 (apart from the specialized units in the key role Manage Energy). They also provide skills development and opportunities for portfolio building.

For a comprehensive list of workbooks, see page ix. For a comprehensive list of links with the standards, see the *User Guide*.

How to use the programme

The programme is deliberately designed to be flexible and can be used in a variety of ways:

- to update on important management topics and themes, or develop individual skills: as the workbooks are grouped according to themes, it should be easy for you to pick out one that suits your needs

- as part of generic management development programmes: you can choose the modules that fit the themes of the programme

■   as part of, and in support of, accredited competence-based programmes.

For N/SVQs at both Levels 4 and 5, there are options in the combinations of units that make up the various awards. By using the map provided in the *User Guide*, individuals will be able to select the workbooks appropriate to their specific needs, and their chosen accreditation options. Some of the activities will help you provide evidence for your portfolio; where we think this is the case, we give the relevant reference to the standards.

For Certificate or CMS, Diploma or DMS, individuals should choose modules that not only meet their individual needs but also satisfy the requirements of the delivering body and the awarding body.

You may need help and guidance in these choices, and the *User Guide* sets out the options and advice in much more detail. A fuller description of the potential uses of this material in evidence gathering and portfolio building can also be found in the *User Guide*, as can a detailed description of the contents of each workbook.

Workbooks in the Institute of Management Open Learning Programme

Personal Competences (Levels 4 and 5)

   1 *The Influential Manager**
   2 *Managing Yourself**

Manage Activities (Level 4)

   3 *Understanding Business Process Management*
   4 *Customer Focus*

Manage Activities (Level 5)

   5 *Getting TQM to Work*
   6 *Leading from the Front*
   7 *Improving Your Organization's Success*

Manage Resources (Level 4)

   8 *Project Management*
   9 *Budgeting and Financial Control*

Manage Resources (Level 5)

10 *Effective Financial and Resource Management*

Manage People (Level 4)

   1 *The Influential Manager*
   2 *Managing Yourself*
11 *Getting the Right People to do the Right Job*
12 *Developing Yourself and Your Staff*
13 *Building a High Performance Team*

An asterisk indicates that a particular workbook also contains material suitable for a particular key role or personal competence over and above that where it is principally designated.

Links to qualifications

S/NVQ programmes

This workbook can help candidates to achieve credit and develop skills in the key role Manage Information at Level 4, and covers the following units and elements:

D4 Provide information to support decision making

D4.1 Obtain information for decision making

D4.2 Record and store information

D4.3 Analyse information to support decision making

D4.4 Advise and inform others

Certificate and Diploma programmes

This workbook, together with the other Level 4 workbook on Manage Information (*Communication*) covers all of the knowledge required in the key role Manage Information for Certificate in Management and CMS programmes.

Links to other workbooks

The other workbook in the key role Manage Information at Level 4 is:

16 *Communication*

and at Level 5:

17 *Successful Information Management*

Introduction

Managers are expected to take decisions. It is what they are there to do. As a middle manager, you will take some decisions of your own – and also collect and organize information to allow people who are more senior to you in the organization to make other decisions.

This book is designed to help you contribute to this process more effectively. But it begins by asking whether you may be taking too many decisions. A lot of decisions go wrong because they are taken at the wrong time, and some because they should not be taken at all.

There are several ways of coming to a decision. For example, you can follow existing guidelines, or make a snap judgement, or work things out logically. Each of these methods is appropriate in some situations and you will be encouraged to apply the best method in the circumstances you are facing. In this book we will examine the types of decisions and decision situations that arise in working life. We will set out some ideas on types and sources of information and we will set out some methods for dealing with problems and making decisions. Finally, we will examine how to communicate decisions with others who have a vested interest in them!

Objectives

By the end of this workbook you should be able to:

- Establish systems and relationships to provide information
- Determine information requirements, and develop questioning skills to find out information
- Establish systems to manage, store and retrieve information
- Make decisions based on information analysis
- Communicate information and decisions

Section 1　Decisions

The verb 'decide' is derived from two Latin words meaning 'to cut off from'. A decision is, quite literally, a cut-off point. It is the moment at which we draw a line under controversy and doubt and are free to move forward in a new direction. Before we take a decision, we are often at our most confused and vulnerable, and the more we consider the possible consequences of the various courses of action we could take, the more irresolute we may feel. Once we have taken a decision, however, most of us experience a sense of relief and liberation.

The ability to take good decisions is an attractive quality. It feels uncomfortable when we are uncertain about the future and we are often grateful to the person who is able to rescue us from this situation. A manager who can provide a strong sense of direction will gain the confidence and support of his or her colleagues. Indeed, people sometimes think of 'decisiveness' as a moral attribute, like 'courage' or 'integrity', which individual managers either have or haven't got. But the capacity to take decisions in which you, and those around you, can have confidence, is a skill which can be acquired. In this first section we will begin to explore how you can do this.

Avoiding unnecessary decisions

Some managers like to show how decisive they are by taking as many decisions as possible. You've probably come across colleagues who don't feel they are doing their job properly unless they take three or four major decisions before breakfast. Managers of this type tend to have a high profile within the organization. But the number of decisions they take is not necessarily any indication of the quality of their judgement.

The first thing that a skilled decision maker must do is to recognize when there is a decision to be taken – and when there isn't. There are several types of situations in which you may be asked to make your mind up about something, but should probably hold back:

- when you are faced with a problem, not a decision
- when the decision only arises because a new option has appeared
- when the decision is connected to another, apparently more important decision which you have just taken
- when you are not the best person to take the decision
- when the time is not right

DECISIONS AND PROBLEMS

Frequently, something that is presented as a decision is actually not a decision at all, but a problem. It is important to understand the difference between these two, because they need to be handled in quite different ways.

- ■ If you have a situation where something is not proceeding as it should, this is a problem
- ■ If you have a have a situation where you must choose from a range of options, this is a decision

It is very easy to confuse decisions with problems, especially if they are described to you by someone else. Read this example:

My assistant came to me and said, 'Jane is coming to the end of her contract next month. I've been rather disappointed with the results she's produced. We could give her another six months, but I don't think we should renew her contract. What do you think?'

On the face of it, this looks like a decision. Only two options are offered:

- ■ give Jane another six month contract
- ■ don't renew Jane's contract

However, what you really have here is a problem:

- ■ Jane is not producing the results which she was expected to achieve

Treat a problem like this:

1   Define the boundaries of the problem
    How long has Jane been under-performing?
    Is she under-performing in all areas of her job, or just some areas?
2   Identify the causes of the problem
    Is Jane ill, or perhaps going through a period of stress at home?
    Has she received adequate training?
    Are there other factors at work that make it impossible for her to do her job properly?
3   Once you know the cause, devise a range of alternative actions to deal with the problem
    If Jane has not received adequate training, the options could be:

- ■ give Jane another six month contract and hope she gets up to speed
- ■ give Jane another contract and provide her with some relevant training
- ■ don't give Jane another contract, but make sure that her replacement receives adequate training

■ replace Jane with someone who has already received appropriate training

Now there really is a decision to be taken.

ACTIVITY 1

Put yourself in the position of the manager who was asked whether Jane should have another contract. If you restricted yourself to the two options that were originally presented – and failed to discover that this was a problem caused by lack of training, what could the consequences to the organization be of:

1   renewing Jane's contract?

2   not renewing Jane's contract?

FEEDBACK

1   You may be lucky. Jane could gain in experience and improve her performance without training. On the other hand, she may not. In this case, she will continue to under-achieve.
2   You may have missed an opportunity to develop Jane into a valuable employee. You will certainly be involved in the expense of finding a replacement. And if you are not aware of the importance of training, you may well make the same mistake with her replacement.

If you take a decision when you really ought to be solving a problem, the chances are that the problem will not go away.

DECISIONS AND DIVERSIONS

From time to time, you will have read advertisements like these:

Can your business survive without....?

Act now and save 50% on your .... bills!

Don't renew your .... until you've talked to us.

Dramatic and alarming statements of this kind are intended to stop you in your tracks. The people who make them are trying to get you to consider the product, service, idea or proposal that they are promoting. They want you to think they are making an offer you can't refuse. The benefits often appear extremely attractive, and the dangers of ignoring the option can seem frightening. It is often very tempting to explore these possibilities.

ACTIVITY 2

Imagine that you are driving across country to an important meeting that will start in an hour's time, along a route you have travelled several times before. You are thirty miles from your destination and the road is clear ahead of you. You see a signpost pointing up a narrow side road that you haven't noticed on earlier journeys. It indicates twenty miles to your destination. Would you:

1   turn into the side road without further thought?

2   ignore the side road and continue on your existing route?

3   stop the car, consult a map and then decide whether to drive up the side road?

Why?

FEEDBACK

You would be foolish to take the side road in these circumstances. The risk of getting lost would not be worth the benefit of arriving slightly early for your meeting. Most people would not even stop the car to consult a map and check where the side road went. The delay to the journey this would involve would not be balanced by any useful benefit.

If you know where you are going – and are confident of getting there – it is not usually worth taking a diversion from your planned route to embark on a mystery tour. When you have started on a course of action at work and a new option is presented to you, ask yourself this question:

If I ignore this option, will I achieve my objectives anyway?

If your answer is yes, you don't have to spend your time making a decision about the new option. If your answer is no, recognize that you are faced with a problem, not a decision. You need to look at your problem carefully and assemble a range of options to choose from.

Sometimes, a new option can seem so extremely attractive that you feel obliged to investigate it further, even though it is not essential to the achievement of your objectives. In this situation, consider carefully whether the benefits are actually of value to you. This may seem obvious – but how often have you been persuaded to buy something you didn't really want because you couldn't resist a special offer? If the benefits *are* of potential value to you, remember that there will also be costs and risks associated with the proposed option – and you may not get unbiased information about these from the person who has brought the option to your attention. If, and only if, you can afford the time to get an objective opinion on the new alternative, then it may be worth considering further.

You do not have to spend time coming to a decision about every new option that appears. The people who are trying to persuade you know this – which is why they try very hard indeed to get your attention so that you will think about the option they are promoting. Be open to innovative ideas – but consider them on your own terms, when the situation demands it.

BIG DECISIONS AND LITTLE DECISIONS

When you have made a big decision about something, you often find that you are asked to make other, smaller decisions immediately afterwards. For example, if you have purchased an expensive piece of equipment, you may be asked if you want to sign a service agreement. When you have booked a holiday, you may be offered insurance. These subsidiary decisions can appear insignificant in the wake of the major decision you have just taken. Beware! It is at this point that you are at your most vulnerable. Many people feel so relieved at having decided the main issue that their judgement is temporarily suspended. You may not be getting nearly such a good bargain on these 'extras' as you did on the original deal. Experienced salespeople know this and many companies have a much higher mark-up on these supplementary items.

A similar thing can happen in any type of negotiation. Once you have agreed a major decision, don't be tempted to clear up all the smaller details immediately. You will probably make better decisions if you wait.

IS THIS MY DECISION?

Don't waste your time by trying to take other people's decisions for them. It is important to recognize when a decision is at too high a level for you, and pass it on to the relevant individual within the organization.

ACTIVITY 3

Give three examples of decisions that you would refer to a senior manager within your organization.

1

2

3

Do these decisions have anything in common?

FEEDBACK

Senior managers are usually responsible for taking strategic decisions while middle managers are responsible for decisions related to the implementation of strategy. The examples you identified are likely to involve situations in which you were uncertain how to apply the organization's strategy, or which were not covered by it, or where the strategy clearly wasn't working. Your examples could also have been decisions for which there wasn't a precedent, or where the consequences of getting things wrong were potentially serious for the organization.

If you refer a decision to a higher authority, you will probably be asked to describe the options and perhaps to make a recommendation. Techniques that you can use to communicate information to decision makers are explored in the final section of this book.

You may also be tempted to take operational decisions that really ought to be the responsibility of people at a lower level than yourself in the organization. This can happen if:

- you don't trust the people whom you are managing to make the right decisions
- your subordinates are frightened of making the wrong decisions
- accepted procedure says that you have to make these decisions
- you are worried about diminishing the area of your authority

ACTIVITY 4

Think about the decisions that the people whom you manage regularly refer to you. What decisions could they handle themselves:

if they had more skills and experience?

if they had more confidence?

if the system allowed them to?

if you were willing to let them?

FEEDBACK

If you could think of some decisions in any of these categories, it may be that you need to develop the skills or confidence of the people you manage, or make recommendations for changes in the decision-making structure of your organization.

Giving the people you manage more responsibility for decisions can be a way of empowering them – and so increasing their commitment to what they are doing. You can read about how to go about developing and empowering your staff in Workbooks 12 and 13.

LETTING GO

When you have set a project or a process underway, there comes a time when you ought to stand back and let things happen. The more decisions you have taken beforehand, the more difficult it can be to stop making decisions when events are underway.

On the day of an important presentation, I was like a cat on a hot tin roof. Should I introduce a second coffee break? Perhaps I should change the order of my OHPs? Should I give the media packs out before the presentation or afterwards? A colleague had to take me aside and say, 'Look, you've been planning every detail of this event for months. It's going to be fine. Just relax, stop worrying and stop trying to make last minute changes.'

If your preparation has been thorough, there comes a point when you have to stop making decisions and allow things to take their course.

Many projects and processes take a little time to settle down and you can expect some anomalous results at first. You can often do much more harm than good by taking unnecessary decisions in the early stages. Be aware of the parameters within which you can safely allow events to vary from your plan, and don't interfere unless they exceed these limits. The period you wait before making new decisions will clearly depend on the kind of activity you are managing. If you are in charge of a satellite launch, you will only have seconds to monitor the trajectory of the rocket and decide whether to abort the mission. But if you are in charge of a publicity campaign that is not bringing in the expected orders, you may have several days or even weeks before a decision is necessary.

GETTING THE TIMING RIGHT

Shakespeare recognized the tragic consequences that await decision makers who get their timing wrong. Hamlet was a classic case of indecision. He spent five acts of the play agonizing about whether he should avenge the murder of his father. It was only in the final scene that Hamlet did the deed and despatched his father's killer. By this point, things had got so out of hand that most of the main characters in the play were dead – and Hamlet himself was dying from a dose of poison.

King Lear went to the other extreme. In the first scene of the play he announced his early retirement and his plan to divide his kingdom among his three daughters. When his favourite daughter didn't react in the way he expected, he made a snap decision to cut her off without a penny. As a result of this momentary lack of judgement, Lear descended into madness, the country was torn apart by war and most of the people in the play came to unpleasant ends.

ACTIVITY 5

Are you a Hamlet or a King Lear? Have you ever let a situation deteriorate because you were unable to take a decision, or taken an unwise decision in the heat of the moment?

If so, what were the consequences?

FEEDBACK

If you recognized a tendency within yourself to take decisions either too slowly or too quickly, be aware of the damaging consequences that this can have. If you erred in either direction (and most people have at some time or another), you should find the decision-making techniques described in this book helpful.

It is not a good idea to take a decision when you are angry. Other emotions can distort your judgement, too:

I felt so grateful for his support that I agreed to sign the contract immediately.

I decided to withdraw the formal warning on the spot because I felt sympathetic about the problems he was experiencing.

I was really disappointed about the way my proposal was received and I decided not to put it before the Board.

I only made that statement to the press because I was shocked at what had happened.

I was so embarrassed by the way the customer had been treated that I over-reacted when I spoke to the member of staff who had been involved.

Try not to make a decision when you are emotionally involved in the situation. If circumstances permit, wait until you feel more detached.

Dealing with difficult decisions

If you know you've got to take an important decision, you may feel very uncomfortable. The more serious the consequences of the decision, the more uneasy you are likely to feel. Some people find these periods of uncertainty quite intolerable and react by rushing the decision, before they have the necessary information.

The pressure to make a quick decision can come from three sources:

- from your own desire to get the decision over with
- from the people who will be affected by the decision who want to know where they stand
- from the situation itself

If the pressure comes from either of the first two sources, set a time or a date when you will make the decision, and, if relevant, tell the people involved.

I had to decide whether or not to fund a project which had been proposed by someone in my department. She was on tenterhooks about the result and was asking me about it every day. It was a good project and I was pretty sure I would agree to the funding she had asked for. However, I knew I should not make a decision until I had discussed the matter with two independent experts whom I had asked to comment on her proposal. I told her that nothing would be decided until the beginning of next month, when I would be able to give her my verdict. She was a bit disappointed at first, but then her anxiety seemed to evaporate and she was able to concentrate on her work.

However, if the circumstances themselves demand that you make a quick decision, don't put it off. Some decisions really do have to be made immediately. They may not be the decisions that you would most like to have behind you, or the ones which other people are pressing you to take. They may not even be the decisions where the consequences are particularly important.

You need to be able to distinguish between decisions that are important, and decisions that are urgent. A decision can be urgent without being particularly important. It can also be important without being urgent. A few decisions are both urgent and important. We'll look at how to handle these different kinds of decision later in the section.

The next activity asks you to bring together the ideas you have met in the first part of this section.

ACTIVITY 6

List the last ten decisions you made at work, regardless of their size or importance. For each decision, consider whether you really needed to make it, or whether the decision could have been handled in some other way. Perhaps it could have been dealt with by someone else. Or perhaps there was not a decision to be made at all.

	Decision	**Alternative ways of dealing with it**
1		
2		
3		
4		
5		
6		
7		
8		
9		
10		

FEEDBACK

You may have considered that most of your decisions were necessary and could only have been taken by you at the time at which you took them. But if you identified *any* decisions that you need not have taken, write this number as a percentage. One decision out of ten = ten per cent. Two decisions = twenty per cent, and so on. On average, how much time do you think you waste taking unnecessary decisions?

Any time that you spend on unnecessary decisions would be better used taking the decisions which really matter. With a clearer desk, and a clearer mind, you will be able to give these decisions the attention they deserve.

Types of decision

A decision can require an answer that is:

- off-the-peg, or
- tailor-made

We'll look at the characteristics of each of these types of decision.

OFF-THE-PEG DECISIONS

These are the routine decisions for which clear criteria exist. The same decision, or something very like it, has already been taken. The consequences of these decisions can be relatively trivial, or very important indeed for the people who are affected, but there is not usually much argument about which way they should go.

A salesperson does not require a detailed knowledge of tailoring to sell an off-the-peg suit. Similarly, off-the-peg decisions can be taken by people who do not have the skill, experience or authority to make the decisions single-handed. For example, a receptionist at a hotel desk can refer to the organization's policy when deciding not to accept a cheque without a supporting credit card. Other off-the-peg decisions are so cut and dried that they can be handled by a machine. For example, a hole-in-the-wall cash machine at a bank uses the following criteria to decide whether to dispense money:

1   Does the owner of the card have an account with this bank, or a bank with which we have an arrangement?
2   Does the account holder have sufficient funds in his or her account?
3   If not, has an overdraft facility been agreed?
4   Does the PIN number correspond with the cash card?
5   Has the card been reported lost or stolen?

If the answer to the first four questions is yes, and the answer to the last question is no, the machine will dispense money.

Some decisions cannot be reduced to a clear procedure involving a series of 'yes/no' questions, but an off-the-peg solution is still available. For example, imagine that a member of your staff has asked if he can download an item of software from the office network onto his own laptop, so that he can continue a piece of work at home. In making your decision, you would be probably be guided by:

- how you have treated similar requests in the past
- the organization's written or unwritten policy about transferring software
- the legal requirements of the software licence
- the expert opinion of the network manager

ACTIVITY 7

Think of an off-the-peg decision that you have made recently. What was it?

What did you use to help you make your decision?

FEEDBACK

Even if you don't know what to do immediately when you are faced with an off-the-peg decision, the answer is not usually difficult to find. Somebody has already thought about this situation and can provide you with guidance.

At some point in its history, every off-the-peg decision was a tailor-made decision. Somebody had to write the guidelines and lay down the criteria. We'll describe some techniques you can use to do this later in the book.

TAILOR-MADE DECISIONS

These are the decisions where no easy precedent or policy exists for you to follow. You have to make up your own mind by assembling and evaluating a list of options. Tailor-made decisions take longer to make and there is undoubtedly more room for error. They are, however, infinitely more satisfying for the decision maker and are more likely to produce an appropriate answer. Most of the rest of this book is devoted to how to make decisions of this kind.

Seven ways to make your mind up

There are several ways to make a decision, and you have probably used them all at one time or another:

- making a random choice
- following tradition
- going by the book
- going by experience
- gut feelings
- trial and error
- logical reasoning

There are some circumstances in which each of these methods can be appropriate.

MAKING A RANDOM CHOICE

If you are in a situation where:

- you have to make a decision quickly in order to move on to the next stage, AND
- the consequences are not important, AND
- you have no idea which option to choose

making a random choice is not a bad way to make your mind up.

We were rushing to get a report ready for a meeting. My assistant came to me with two versions of the cover. One was printed on shiny white card and the other on matt grey card. They both looked good – I would have been happy with either version. There was no point in making a meal of the decision, so I just picked up the one which was nearest to me on the desk and said, 'We'll go with this one.'

The big advantage of this method is its speed. It is appropriate in situations where the swiftness of the decision is more important than the potential consequences of the various options. It is not appropriate in situations where making the wrong choice could have serious outcomes.

FOLLOWING TRADITION

Routine, off-the-peg decisions are often made in this way.

We've always sent our best customers a desk diary in December, so let's do the same this year.

None of the women in the office wear trousers to work, so please come in a skirt tomorrow.

Some traditions are valuable, but others just acquire a spurious authority because they have been going on for so long. People can get so used to 'the way things are done round here' that they don't even realize that they are taking a decision to act in a particular way. Following tradition does not guarantee that you will make a good decision, especially if circumstances have changed since the tradition was established. When you make a traditional choice, people will be familiar with what happens next. This may be an advantage or a disadvantage.

ACTIVITY 8   C3.8

Think about your own experience as a manager. Give an example of a time when:

- you followed tradition when you made a decision

- you broke with tradition when you made a decision

In each case, explain why you decided to follow (or break with) tradition.

FEEDBACK

Compare your answers with the following:

Following tradition
I had to choose where to hold the annual office party. I looked at several venues, but in the end I chose the same restaurant that we have used for the last five years. The staff there know us and the arrangements have always worked well in the past. It seemed the safest thing to do.

Breaking with tradition
When I started this job I found that the weekly departmental meetings were often a complete waste of time, so I decided only to call a meeting when we needed to get together. My reason for doing this was obviously to save time, and also to demonstrate that I valued my own time, and the time of other people in the department. Because I was new in the job, I suppose I also wanted to show them that I wasn't afraid of doing things differently.

Following tradition can be an appropriate way to make a routine decision, but it is not an effective way of making a tailor-made decision.

GOING BY THE BOOK

This is the method that is used for making many off-the-peg decisions. It involves consulting the written instructions or guidelines that have been produced for the purpose. Used in appropriate circumstances, it is usually perfectly satisfactory. However, if you have ever needed to persuade someone who goes strictly by the book to take a non-routine decision, you will be aware that this method has definite limitations.

I needed to make an urgent phone call from a train. It was a genuine emergency – I had been delayed on my way home from a meeting and needed to arrange child care for my daughter who would shortly be arriving back from school. I hadn't got my mobile with me and both the public phones on the train were out of order. So I asked the buffet steward if I could use his phone. He refused, on the grounds that passengers weren't permitted to use company equipment. I explained my problem but he would not budge. He told me that it was more than his job was worth to let me use that phone. In the end, I borrowed another passenger's mobile phone. I wrote a strong complaint to the train company, complaining about this inflexibility, and received a letter of apology.

It is important to recognize when the book is inadequate, and also to make sure that your staff understand the circumstances in which they should either depart from the guidelines or refer a decision to a higher authority.

GOING BY EXPERIENCE

If you have had the right type of experience, this can be enormously helpful when you have to make a routine decision. You can instantly recognize the criteria to use and which procedures or guidelines apply in the situation. You are also in a good position to make a tailor-made decision, and may not have to go through the process of making a formal comparison of all the various options.

The danger here is that you will not recognize when a decision lies outside your experience.

When I was working for a publishing company, a lot of unsolicited manuscripts arrived on our desks. I normally read the adult fiction, but one day a colleague asked me to take a look at a children's book that someone had sent in. I thought it was complete rubbish and said so in my report. On the basis of my verdict, we rejected the manuscript. The author took it elsewhere. It wasn't an international best-seller, but the author went on to write several books which were. If I hadn't written that report, we would have been his publishers. The mistake I made was to assume that I had the experience to know what type of children's book would appeal to the public, when I really didn't.

ACTIVITY 9

Use this diagram to record the topics about which you have (and have not) the experience to make a decision. If you feel very confident about the relevance of your experience, write the topic near the centre of the circle. If you are less sure, write it near the edge of the circle. If you know that you do not have the experience to make a decision about something, write it outside the circle.

Start by writing the following topics on your diagram, then add some other topics of your own.

health and safety
employment law
staff training
IT

FEEDBACK

If a decision lies outside your experience, it is much better to admit it and get some expert advice from someone who has the relevant experience.

GUT FEELINGS

Sometimes you may get a strong feeling about which way a decision should go, regardless of what the evidence suggests.

One of the candidates for the job looked really good on paper. He had excellent qualifications and an impeccable work record in his CV. And he was charm personified at the interview. But there was something I couldn't put my finger on which made me uneasy...

In a situation like this, you can't go on intuition alone. Begin by considering whether your reaction is due to:

- something about you
- something about the option that you are considering

For example, are you made uneasy by this candidate because he:

- reminds you of somebody at college whom you really disliked?
- has managed to achieve things you would like to have done yourself?
- has eyes that are too close together?
- looks as though he might be up for your job in a couple of years' time?

Examine your own prejudices and fears. If you can honestly say that your gut feeling is not connected to them, then try to work out the source of your uneasiness. We pick up a lot of subconscious messages from the world and many of them are important. In this situation, it could be that:

- the candidate's body language is showing that he is hiding something
- his work record does not follow a normal pattern
- he did not ask a question you would have expected him to ask
- you have heard rumours about difficulties at one of the places he has worked

If you have an irrational feeling against a particular option, this may be a signal that you need to get more information about it. Gut feelings are often an indication that what appears to be a routine decision actually needs to be a tailor-made decision.

TRIAL AND ERROR

This is an expensive way of making decisions. While it makes sense to learn as much as you can from any decision that goes wrong, it is not a good idea actually to invite failure. It is much better to give some extra thought to the decision before you take it.

There is also a difference between learning from your failures and simply reacting to them.

Last year we leased our office equipment from a local company. It was a total disaster. The machines kept going wrong and we had to wait days for an engineer to turn up. The next time, we are definitely going to buy new equipment, not lease it.

The trouble with using the trial and error method is that you are simply reacting to disaster, instead of analysing and learning from it. It could be that the manager who had the bad experience with the leased equipment simply chose the wrong company. The fact that one leasing arrangement was unsuccessful does not necessarily indicate that all similar arrangements must be avoided in the future. When a decision goes wrong, treat the situation as a problem and explore its boundaries and causes. Do not simply take it as a reason to do something different the next time around. Better still, spend more time thinking about the decision before you take it and reduce the likelihood of error.

If you have ever been managed by someone who takes decisions on a trial and error basis, you will know how demotivating it can be. Your confidence in any decisions that are taken is low, as is your commitment to making them work.

Logical reasoning

This is the best way to make tailor-made decisions. It involves examining the implications of a range of options and making a considered choice. This is the method that we shall be exploring in this book. There are five stages to making a rational decision:

- consider
- consult
- crunch
- communicate
- check

Consider

Begin by considering what kind of decision you are dealing with. The ideas discussed in this first section will help you here. Are you sure you really have to make a decision at all? If so, is the decision important, or just urgent? Does it require an off-the-peg or a tailor-made solution? Your answers to these questions will help you decide how much time and effort you should give to making the decision.

Consult

The next stage is to assemble the information you need to make your decision. This may involve simply asking a colleague for his or her opinion – or, at the other extreme, launching a major research project. Techniques you can use for gathering and organizing information are covered in Section 2 of this book. Sometimes you will need to assemble information to help someone

else make a decision. Section 4 looks at ways you can communicate this information to those people who will make the decision.

Crunch

This is the moment at which you analyse and compare the information you
have gathered and actually make the decision. Techniques you can use to
evaluate different options are described in Section 3 of this book.

Communicate

Once you have made your decision, you need to communicate it to the people who will be affected by it. If you don't get this stage right, you can undo
the benefits of making a good decision. Techniques for communicating decisions are discussed in Section 4.

Check

When a decision has been made, you need to monitor and evaluate its effect.
This will inform subsequent decisions. Ways of checking your decisions are
discussed in Section 4.

Making a rational decision takes time and can involve the use of expensive
resources. Although it is the method that is most likely to yield the best result,
it is not appropriate in all circumstances. If you need a quick answer, or the
consequences of making the wrong decision are not serious, you may do better to use one of the other methods.

ACTIVITY 10

Think of two decisions that you have to make in the near future. Which methods will you use to come to these decisions? Why?

Decision 1

Method

Why

Decision 2

Method

Why

Check your answers against these points:

- **Making a random choice**   Do you need to make a quick decision and are the consequences relatively unimportant?
- **Following tradition**   Is the decision routine? What are the benefits of not breaking with tradition here?
- **Going by the book**   Is the decision routine? Are the existing guidelines relevant?
- **Going by experience**   Is your experience relevant?
- **Gut feelings**   Are these due to your own prejudices and fears, or do they have an objective basis?
- **Trial and error**   Are you sure that you have analysed past mistakes and are not simply reacting to them? Is there a better way of making this decision?
- **Logical reasoning**   Is this decision important enough to justify the time and resources you will give to it? Is this a routine decision? If so, consider using another method.

Summary

Now that you have finished this section, you should be able to:

- distinguish between decisions and problems
- avoid decisions that are prompted by the appearance of a new option
- take especial care with 'minor' decisions when you have just taken a 'major' decision
- recognize decisions that should be taken by people at a higher or lower level than you in the organization
- recognize when it is time to let go of a decision
- avoid taking decisions too slowly, or too quickly, or when you are emotionally involved
- distinguish between routine and non-routine decisions
- choose an appropriate method of decision making

Section 2   Gathering and managing information

If you are going to make a rational decision, you need quality information. This is information that is relevant, current, adequate, timely, reliable and cost-effective. In this section you will discover how to recognize information that has these characteristics – and the data sources where you are most likely to find it.

You will be encouraged to try out various techniques to gather primary and secondary data. You will also read about the possibilities offered by other research methods that you may commission at some time in the future.

The section ends by considering issues that you need to think about when you store data and information. These ideas should help you maximize the accessibility of the information you have gathered. They should also make you more aware of how information is handled in your organization.

Data, information and knowledge

These three words are often used as though they mean exactly the same thing, but the difference between them is actually very significant.

- **Data**   These are the undigested facts and figures that are collected on innumerable subjects. You may gather data yourself, or use data that has been gathered by other people.
- **Information**   This comprises data that has been selected and processed for a specific purpose.
- **Knowledge**   This is the understanding that results from bringing together and interpreting different pieces of information.

An individual fact can be data, information or knowledge, depending on the context in which it is held. For example:

- The name and telephone number of a local plumber printed in the *Yellow Pages* are **data**.
- The same name and telephone number, when copied onto a piece of paper in

response to a request for a local plumber, are **information**.

■ The same name and telephone number, when used in association with another piece of information: 'the name of that plumber you used last year who was so good when your boiler broke down', are **knowledge**.

When you are going to make a decision, you need to:

■ gather data

■ select and process the data to give you information

■ process and compare information to produce knowledge

Once you have knowledge, you can make a decision and take action. Figure 1 illustrates the stages involved in making a decision.

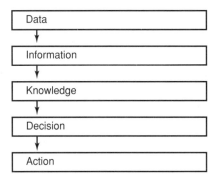

Figure 1   Stages in decision making

Imagine that you want to buy a laptop computer.

1   You get hold of catalogues from four companies that sell equipment of this kind. You now have the relevant **data**.

2   You find laptops that match the specifications you are looking for in each catalogue. You now have **information**.

3   Finally, you compare prices and other features. You now have **knowledge** that you can use to choose the laptop you will buy.

You would probably go through these three stages when choosing a laptop computer. But there is something missing from this process.

ACTIVITY 11

Imagine you were going to buy a laptop computer. What would you actually do first, before you got hold of the catalogues?

The first thing you would probably do is to look at other people's laptops to get a general idea of what was available and the features that were important to you.

This first stage is absolutely crucial. In it, you are beginning to identify the criteria you will use to make your final decision. You need to know these criteria in order to select your information. You also need to know what information you are looking for when you gather your data. As Figure 2 shows, the process really works backwards!

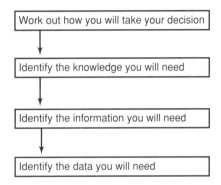

Figure 2   Process of decision making

The first section of the book concentrated on decisions. You were encouraged to think about which kinds of decision merit serious research and deliberation – and which kinds you can take in other ways. Actual decision-making techniques, which help you to analyse and compare various options, turning information into knowledge, are explored in Section 3. In this section we will be looking at how to gather data and transform it into information.

Quality information

Quality information is fit for purpose. The purpose is dictated by the decision you are going to take. Clearly, different types of decision will require different types of information. However, there are certain general characteristics that you can look for in the information you select. It must be:

- relevant
- current
- adequate
- timely
- reliable
- cost-effective

We'll look at each of these characteristics in turn.

RELEVANT INFORMATION

The information you select must be relevant to the criteria you are going to use to make your decision. This means that it should:

- tell you what you need to know
- not tell you what you don't need to know

Irrelevant information can waste your time and confuse your decision.

I was trying to choose a hotel for a small conference. I asked my secretary to phone round and see what the choice was in the area. Two days later, she presented me with a dozen glossy brochures. I spent a morning looking through them, staring at pictures of swimming pools, restaurants, gyms and landscaped gardens – and reading about simultaneous translation facilities and videoconferencing suites. I was wondering whether I preferred a sauna or a Jacuzzi and whether it was better to have an à la carte or buffet lunch. Then I suddenly came to my senses. All I really needed was a room which would hold 50 people, a video, a rostrum and a flip chart, with access to a reasonably priced restaurant at lunchtime. Everything else was irrelevant.

If you are clear about the criteria you will use to make your decision, you should find it easier to avoid being side-tracked by irrelevant information.

CURRENT INFORMATION

You need information that is relevant to the existing situation – not some situation that existed in the past. Your information should be obtained from data that is as up-to-date as possible. Most data has a limited shelf life.

ACTIVITY 12

Would you consider that these types of data were useable?

	yes	no
1 Last year's catalogue from an office equipment supplier		
(a) if you were working out the budget for re-equipping the office	❏	❏
(b) if you were working out a new layout for the desks and filing cabinets in the office	❏	❏
2 A six-month-old copy of a trade journal		
(a) if you were deciding whether to accept an invitation to be interviewed by the journal	❏	❏
(b) if you wanted to place an advertisement	❏	❏
3 Last year's copy of an expensive yearbook produced by your industry's trade association		
(a) if you were choosing key figures in the industry to invite to a presentation	❏	❏
(b) if you wanted to check the details of an industrial safety initiative described in the yearbook	❏	❏

FEEDBACK

1 (a) No, because the prices would probably have changed.

(b) Here you would only be interested in the dimensions of the items, which would be unlikely to have changed. So last year's catalogue would be OK.

2 (a) Assuming the journal has not undergone a change of editorial policy, this would probably give you the information you needed.

(b) No, because advertising rates may have changed in the last six months.

3 (a) No, because these key figures may not still be in the same jobs.

(b) You could certainly use the out-of-date yearbook to check the details of the initiative, but you would also be wise to consult a current copy for updated information.

It is usually cheaper and more convenient to use the data you have to hand, rather than search out new data. In some circumstances, old data can still yield valuable information. In other situations, it can be worse than useless.

ADEQUATE INFORMATION

You need information that covers all the criteria you will use to make your decision.

ACTIVITY 13

Imagine that you were going to buy a house in a new area. List ten things that you would want to know about a house before you gave it serious consideration. Tick any of these things that you could find out from the estate agent's information. How would you find out the other things?

1

2

3

4

5

6

7

8

9

10

FEEDBACK

Your list will not be the same as this, but it should reflect your individual requirements in a similar way:

1 number of bedrooms ✓

2 size of rooms ✓

3 how much sun the house gets (visit house at various times of day, talk to owners)

4 state of decoration (visit house)

5 whether there is a good pub within walking distance (visit area)

6 structural condition of house (survey)

7 proximity of public transport ✓

8 quality of local schools (visit schools, talk to local parents)

9 whether there is room for an Aga in the kitchen (visit house)

10 whether the neighbours would object to you practising your trumpet (talk to neighbours)

As this Activity demonstrated, you may need to obtain your information from several different sources. In this situation, the estate agent has prepared the details with the average buyer in mind. He or she cannot know all your individual requirements. Don't assume that you will get all the information you need from the individual or organization that is trying to persuade you to choose the product or service offered.

ACTIVITY 14

What information might you need if you were considering a job application for a post in your team? And where could you get this information?

Information   **Source**

FEEDBACK

Compare your answer with this:

Information	Source
academic qualifications	cv/application form
previous experience	cv/application form, discussion at interview
ability to do the job	discussion at interview, psychometric tests, references
communication skills	cv/application form, impression given at interview

When you are drawing up a list of options, you may not need very detailed information. Later, when you are making your final decision, it may be necessary to go into greater depth.

I wanted to buy a house which would not require much money spent on it. To start with, I ruled out any property which the estate agent described as 'in need of renovation' or 'ripe for improvement'. When I visited houses, I looked out for tell-tale cracks in the plaster and bulging walls. And when I actually chose a house, I brought in my own surveyor to do a full structural survey.

TIMELY INFORMATION

You need information at the point at which you are going to use it, not at some future date. This can affect the type of data you use, and the source you get that data from.

I didn't have the time to wade through a lot of technical details, so I just read the summary at the beginning of the report.

I had to find out as much as possible about an organization before the meeting that afternoon, so I did a search on the Internet.

You often have to strike a balance between time, cost and quality. If you can't get the information you need in order to make a decision at the time you want it, the following options may be open to you:

- pay a financial premium to get the information faster
- make your decision on the basis of inadequate information
- delay your decision until the appropriate information is available

If you choose the first option, you sacrifice money. If you choose the second you sacrifice quality. If you choose the third, you sacrifice time.

ACTIVITY 15

Think of a situation in which you couldn't get the information to make a decision at the time you wanted it.

What did you do? Why?

FEEDBACK

Your answer may be similar to one of these:

'I needed to look at some design drawings to decide what line I would take at a meeting. They hadn't arrived in the morning post, so I arranged for them to be biked over to me. The meeting was important, so the extra cost was well worth it.'

'I had to decide which of three projects I would back. The decision would be affected by changes expected in the Budget. I couldn't get advance information of what the Chancellor would say, so I had no choice but to delay the decision.'

'A customer had complained that a product had been contaminated. I sent the sample to the lab for analysis, but their tests were going to take a few days. There was no way of hurrying these tests. However, I had a strong suspicion that the contaminant had come from a particular machine on the production line. Because the consequences were potentially serious, I decided to act on inadequate information and close the line for overhaul.'

What you do in a situation such as that described above depends on the urgency of the decision and whether its importance justifies paying extra to get information more quickly. Sometimes you have to make such a quick decision that you cannot afford the time to get any but the most basic information. And in some situations it is not possible to get information more quickly by paying more for it.

RELIABLE INFORMATION

You need to be able to trust your information. When you look at a piece of information, ask these questions:

- Has it been put together by someone who really understands the decision and its implications?
- Is there any reason why anyone should try to mislead you?
- Are there any other barriers to getting accurate information?

Darrell Huff wrote a classic book in the 1950s called *How to Lie with Statistics*. This drew attention to many ways in which statistical data can give a misleading impression of reality. He describes two surveys that took place in an area of China. The first survey gave the population as 28 million. Five years later, another survey gave a figure of 105 million for the same area. The enormous difference between these two figures could largely be explained by the way these two surveys were conducted. The first was for tax and military purposes, and the second was for famine relief.

In these days of spin doctors and media management, people have become expert at presenting information in a way that favours their own cause. If you suspect that you are not getting an objective view on the situation, try to go back to the original data and draw your own conclusions.

COST-EFFECTIVE INFORMATION

When you make a decision, you have to balance the benefits of getting the right information against its costs.

ACTIVITY 16

1   You want to purchase a new filing cabinet for your non-confidential papers. What could be the cost of choosing the wrong cabinet?

2   You have been asked to decide whether a letter dismissing a member of staff should be sent out in its present form. What could be the cost of making the wrong decision?

FEEDBACK

Here are some of possible costs of choosing the wrong filing cabinet:

- reduced efficiency if it becomes difficult to get access to your papers
- cost of replacement filing cabinet
- cost of removing the wrong filing cabinet

If you spot your mistake quickly, your costs will not be much more than the price of a replacement cabinet.

However, if you make the wrong decision about the letter of dismissal, you could find that your organization is involved in paying for the staff time, legal fees, bad publicity and compensation payments of a case for wrongful dismissal. These costs could easily amount to many thousands of pounds.

It is clearly worth investing much more in the decision about the letter than in the decision about the filing cabinet.

You should also consider the potential benefits of making the right decision. These will probably come into one of these categories:

- efficiency: achieving a level of performance with less resources
- effectiveness: improving the level of performance with the same resources
- strategic advantage: changing processes and achieving improved overall effectiveness

Some of these benefits can be measured reasonably easily by, for example:

- lower costs
- increased profits
- higher output

Other benefits are more difficult to measure, but still have an important effect. They could include:

- improved staff morale
- increased customer satisfaction
- the fact that you have more time to spend on investigating new projects, resulting in future benefits to the organization

ACTIVITY 17

Think of a decision you have to make soon.

What are the potential costs of making the wrong decision?

What are the potential benefits of making the right decision?

FEEDBACK

This Activity will have given you an indication of the importance of the decision, and hence the resources it is worth using to get it right.

So what are the costs of getting the right information? They are made up of:

- the cost of the information itself, including fees for using a database, consultancy fees, cost of books, magazine and journal subscriptions and conference fees
- the cost of staff time
- lost opportunity costs of other more profitable activities that could have been undertaken instead

ACTIVITY 18

You are considering whether to send one of your staff on a two-day training course that you believe will help him or her to make better decisions on the computer software requirements of your organization. The fees for the course are £250. You will also have to pay accommodation and travel costs of £150.

Work out the cost of staff time for a member of your own team.

Cost of two days' time

$$= \frac{\text{annual salary } + \text{ employer's pension and NI contributions}}{48 \times 5} \times 2$$

Now work out the lost opportunity costs. Is there any work that would result in direct financial gains to the organization and which would not get done if this member of staff was away for two days? If so, estimate its value.

Finally, work out the total cost of sending the person on the training course.

FEEDBACK

You may not have been able to work out this calculation using exact figures, but you probably found that the actual cost of the training and accommodation fees amounted to less than half of the total cost of sending someone on this course.

In order to be cost-effective, the cost of getting any information must clearly be less than the benefits of making a good decision, or the costs of making a bad decision. Suppose that you completed the last Activity on someone who receives salary and other benefits from the organization totalling £20 000 a year and who generates profits of £40 000 a year from his or her activities. Unless there was a strong likelihood that sending him or her on the course would save the organization more than £1000, it could not be justified on financial grounds. There may, however, be other benefits, such as increasing staff loyalty by showing a commitment to training, which you could set against the costs of this exercise.

Quantitative and qualitative information

There are two basic types of information. Quantitative information is expressed in figures. It answers questions such as:

- how much?
- how many?
- how frequently?
- how likely?
- how quickly?

Qualitative information is concerned with things that cannot be measured in numerical terms. It answers questions such as:

- what?
- why?
- how?

Quantitative information is usually obtained from analysing large amounts of numerical data. It is objective, in that you are likely to get the same information, no matter who analyses the figures.

ACTIVITY 19

Think of six pieces of quantitative information that you know about your organization. (You don't have to give the exact figures.)

1

2

3

4

5

6

FEEDBACK

Your examples could be similar to these:

- annual profit or loss
- number of employees
- average wage levels
- number of women employed
- average age of retirement
- average salary levels
- number of branches
- amount of dividend paid to shareholders
- area of office space
- production levels

Now imagine that a friend is considering applying for a job in your organization and asks you for information about it. You might give him or her some figures similar to those you listed in the last activity. But you would also give some qualitative information:

It's a family business that's been making packaging materials since about 1890. It's run on very traditional lines and I think it's going to have to wake up a bit if it's going to survive into the next century. I think there are big changes on the way.

They are a great bunch of people in the company, really committed, and some of them are exceptionally talented. I was very lucky to get a job with them. Haven't regretted it for a moment. You'd love it there, I'm sure. Go for it!

Qualitative information is subjective. It reflects the knowledge and perspective of the individual who provides it. It gives you depth, while quantitative information gives you breadth. There are times when each type of information is useful.

ACTIVITY 20

You have to make decisions about the following things. Would you go for qualitative or quantitative information?

		qualitative	quantitative
1	Which of two styles of illustration to use in a book for young children?	❑	❑
2	Which products to drop from your portfolio?	❑	❑
3	Which candidate to appoint to a job on the assembly line?	❑	❑

FEEDBACK

1 You would discuss the two styles of illustration with people who had experience of the market. You might also show them to a small group of parents and ask for their reactions. In either case, you would receive qualitative information.

2 This decision could be made on the basis of quantitative information alone – by checking the sales figures and production costs. You might also consult someone with knowledge of the market to confirm your decision and he or she might give you some qualitative information, such as 'The only other producer of this item has just closed the factory. You might find there's a growth in demand, so I'd hang in there for a little longer.'

3 If you made the appointment solely on performance in a test, you would be using quantitative data. If you took other things into account, such as the impression that the applicant made at interview, you would also be using qualitative data.

TRANSFORMING QUALITATIVE DATA INTO INFORMATION

By definition, qualitative data consists of facts that are not measured. This can mean that there is no easy way to check this data. You have to rely on the accuracy and adequacy of your source. As a consequence, you must select your source with care, and also be prepared to ask the right questions.

ACTIVITY 21

In each of the following situations, decide whether the data source is adequate and accurate. If it isn't, what other source could you use?

1   You want to write to the research and development manager of a company to discuss the possibility of setting up a project with your own organization. You ask a friend who used to work there for his name. He says, 'It's Hammer. Or Hanner. No, it's definitely Hanner, Richard Hanner. Or was it Michael? I'm almost positive it's Hanner, but I can't be sure of his first name.'

2   You want to find out some information about a conference centre you are planning to hire for the launch of an up-market new product. It is important that the venue contributes to the sense of quality and style you want to associate with the product. You receive a set of glossy brochures from the centre, in which the accommodation looks sensational.

FEEDBACK

1   This information is neither reliable nor adequate. You need to telephone the manager's secretary and ask for his full name.

2   This information is probably adequate, but it may not be reliable. The accommodation was probably newly decorated for the photographs in the brochures. You need to visit the venue to check on its current appearance, or send someone else with a checklist of points to report back on.

Using questions

When you are getting qualitative information from a source you are talking or writing to, there are different types of questions you can use:

- Closed questions, which require a yes/no answer or an answer from a small range of options, are useful for clarifying details.

    Was the reception area tidy?

    Would you describe him as helpful?

    Did you get the impression that they would come up with the goods?

- Open questions, which cannot be answered in one or two words, are useful if you want your informant to supply more information:

    What were the seminar rooms like?

    What impression did you get of her?

    When do you think they would be able to deliver?

- Probing questions, which ask for more information, are useful if you want to go into further detail.

    So which of the two suites you've described would you actually recommend?

    You say you might book the dining room for special occasions – would you eat there on a regular basis?

There are also some types of questions you should avoid:

- Multiple questions, where the person you are speaking to may be unsure which part to answer, can lead to confusion.

    Is it a well-lit room? Would you say it gets as much light as this room we're in now?

- Leading questions, which suggest that you are expecting a particular answer, may make it difficult for the person you are talking to give you any other reply.

    Don't you think that their facilities are absolutely superb?

If you are interested in developing your questioning and listening skills, you will find Workbook 16 *Communication* useful.

TRANSFORMING QUANTITATIVE DATA INTO INFORMATION

Quantitative data is based on figures. Many people, including some managers, have a natural aversion to numbers. When they see a chart containing figures, they assume that it will be difficult to understand. They may not even attempt to make sense of quantitative data, but rely on somebody else to provide a verbal translation and interpretation.

In order to turn quantitative data into useful information, it is necessary to find patterns and meaning in the figures, by using statistical techniques. Although it is possible to study statistics at a very high level, the basic (and most commonly used) techniques are not beyond the understanding of anyone who has completed their secondary education.

In Section 3 we explore some ways of using statistical methods to make sense of figures.

Primary and secondary data

Once you have an idea of the kind of information you need to make your decision, you can begin collecting data. This can come from two types of source:

- Primary data is gathered by you (or your representatives) for your own purposes. It could include survey results, commissioned reports and notes of meeting with consultants.
- Secondary data has been gathered by other people for their own purposes. It includes, among many other things, journals, published reports, internal sales figures and commercial databases.

ACTIVITY 22

Here are the six characteristics of quality information. In general, would you be more likely to find each of these characteristics in primary or secondary data? Tick the appropriate boxes.

	Primary data	Secondary data
relevant	❑	❑
current	❑	❑
adequate	❑	❑
timely	❑	❑
reliable	❑	❑
cost-effective	❑	❑

FEEDBACK

Primary data is likely to be more directly relevant than secondary data. It will also probably be more current. You may be able to gather adequate data yourself. However, the people who put together secondary data have greater resources available to them and often are able to provide more breadth or depth of coverage than you can manage yourself. If relevant secondary data already exists, it will usually be quicker to use it than to do your own research – so secondary data often provides more timely information. Published data will usually have gone through some sort of checking process, so it is often more reliable than primary data. However, you should be aware of any bias on the part of those who prepared it. Finally, it is usually much cheaper to refer to existing data than to find everything out for yourself. The economy of scale makes secondary data more cost-effective than primary data.

When scientists begin a piece of research, they always begin by searching the literature and finding out about the work that has been done already in the field. This has two benefits:

- it prevents them wasting time unnecessarily repeating work that has already been done
- it provides a context in which their own discoveries can be understood

In most situations where you need to gather data, you should follow this example. Gather secondary data first. Then, if necessary, extend this secondary data with primary data of your own.

SECONDARY DATA

The gathering of secondary data is often described as desk research, because it can be accessed by someone sitting at a desk. It can come from a variety of sources.

ACTIVITY 23

The following list covers the major sources of secondary data. For each source, think of at least one example you have used yourself.

- facts and figures collected by other departments within your organization

- reference books

- commercial databases, available both on-line and on CD-ROM

- journals

- newspapers

- published reports

- government statistics

- trade associations

- trade directories

- business centres and libraries

- research organizations

FEEDBACK

Your list will reflect the nature of your organization, and the work you do within it. If you couldn't think of at least one example for each of these types of source, it might be that you are not using a wide enough range of secondary data. In this case, you should make it a priority to investigate other relevant sources.

Accessing secondary data

There are three keys to accessing data:

1   know what you're looking for
2   use all the clues provided to find your way around
3   don't get side-tracked

It can help to start by writing down a list of questions you need to answer, such as:

- what is the population of Peru?
- what's the GDP?
- is the political situation stable?

This will keep you focused – and may stop you spending time gazing at photographs of Nazca ruins, which may not be particularly relevant to your organization's current interest in Peru.

Most sources of data provide some clues on where you can find the information you need. If you are reading a book, use the index and contents page. If you are looking at a journal, read the abstract at the beginning of an article and scan the sub-headings. Don't read more than you have to.

If you are consulting a computer database, find out appropriate search terms. These may be indexed for you. Different databases and search engines have their own rules, and it is worth spending ten minutes finding out what these rules will allow you to do. For example, if you use one of the search engines on the World Wide Web, you can customize your search by selecting these options:

- match any term
- match all terms
- match 2, 3, 4, etc. terms
- loose/fair/good/close/strong match

You can ask for the results to appear in standard, summary or detailed format. By typing "bank -river" you can specify that you want references to banks that do not contain references to rivers, which could be useful if you were searching for data on banking systems. By typing "med$" you can specify that you want references to any words that start with these letters, such as medicine, medical, medicinal, and so on.

Remember that all search tools are provided to make your life easier. They are not usually difficult to understand, so use them.

ACTIVITY 24

Choose an electronic database with which you are not familiar. Find out how to do a search. Write the instructions down here:

Then do a search for a piece of information that you will need in the near future. How successful were you?

FEEDBACK

Even those managers who are comfortable with accessing data from the Internet or CD-ROMs can get into the habit of using the same sources all the time. You may find that new sites and sources are worth exploring. Also, technology is changing so quickly that you may find that sites and sources that you didn't find particularly easy or profitable to use in the past have now been updated.

PRIMARY DATA

Primary data is data that you collect yourself, or arrange for other people to collect on your behalf. You can do this in a formal way, by using various types of survey, interviewing experts or even setting up a full research project. You can also collect primary data by informal methods, through the use of networking. We'll look at the formal methods first.

Surveys

A survey involves collecting data from a large number of subjects, which can then be analysed statistically. The more subjects you can include in your survey, the more accurate it will be. And the more expensive. You need help from professional researchers and statisticians if you are going to undertake a survey of any real size.

Most surveys involve questionnaires. These can be administered face-to-face, by telephone or in the post. All three methods have their advantages and disadvantages. Table 1, which is reproduced from the Institute of Management Foundation checklist on the subject, outlines the pros and cons.

Table 1 Advantages and disadvantages of questionnaires

	Face-to-face	Telephone	Postal
Acceptability	reasonable	doubtful	open choice
Recruitment	controlled	controlled	self-selecting
Response rate	fixed	fixed	variable
Speed	moderate	fast	slow
Reaching scattered sample	poor	very good	very good
Interaction/rapport	very good	good	poor
Complexity of interview	possible	limited	impossible
Interviewer bias	present	present	absent
Interview length	up to 1 hour (prearranged)	10–15 minutes	30 minutes (max)
Staff resources needed	large	substantial	moderate

ACTIVITY 25

How would you administer the following questionnaires?

		Face-to-face	Telephone	Postal
1	To explore in depth the attitudes of important customers to your services	❏	❏	❏
2	To identify the names of as many people as possible who are worth adding to a mailing list for new product information	❏	❏	❏

FEEDBACK

1 Since you need in-depth information from a small number of people, it would be better to speak to them face-to-face.
2 Here you only need to ask much more basic questions. You are also interested in getting responses from as many people as possible, so a postal questionnaire would be best.

Questionnaires are usually only sent to a sample of people, not to everyone whose views you would like to know. A sample can be random, or based on quotas, which include certain numbers of people who come into different categories, such as males and females, age groups, geographical location or social groups.

Before you write a questionnaire, you should work out what you are going to do with your results. Think how you will analyse your data and whether you want everyone to answer all the questions.

The following checklist contains some points to remember when designing questions.

- Don't ask too many questions. Think how much time the respondent will be prepared to spend on the questionnaire
- Ask easy questions at the beginning, sensitive questions in the middle or at the end and classification questions (such as age group) at the end
- Use a simple, logical structure which will not confuse people
- Avoid leading questions which will influence the answers you get
- Avoid jargon

- Avoid words like 'reasonable' or 'satisfactory' which could be interpreted in many ways
- Avoid multiple questions
- Remember that open questions take much longer to code and analyse – so use them with care

Questionnaires often ask about people's attitudes. The most commonly used types of question here are known as **Likert** and **semantic differential**.

In a Likert question, you write a statement and ask for a response from a range of options such as this:

- strongly agree
- slightly agree
- neither agree nor disagree
- slightly disagree
- strongly disagree

You then give a numerical score (ranging from, for example, 5 to 1) to the answer. If you mix positive and negative statements, such as:

- I enjoy meeting new people
- I dislike talking to people I have just met

you must obviously remember to reverse the scoring system, so that a 'strongly agree' answer to the first question scores the same as a 'strongly disagree' answer to the second one.

In semantic differential questions, you offer respondents a sliding scale between two opposite answers:

Was the receptionist who took your booking:

friendly 1 2 3 4 5 unfriendly?

ACTIVITY 26

Design a question for a questionnaire that would help you find out what customers think of the advertising material produced by your organization.

Check your question against the checklist above. Are you still happy with it?

If you design a questionnaire, make sure to pilot it before you send it out. This should allow you to identify any confusing questions or other problems.

Interviews

An interview can be:

- structured
- semi-structured
- non-structured

A structured interview is the same as a face-to-face questionnaire. The interviewer has a set list of questions to ask and must try not to influence the answers he or she gets. In a semi-structured interview, the interviewer has a set list of topics to cover, but has more freedom about the way he or she asks the questions. In a non-structured interview, the interviewer starts out with topics to cover, but can allow the direction of the interview to change, if the interviewee comes up with other ideas that look as though they are worth exploring. As you move from a structured towards a non-structured format, the influence of the interviewer increases. This has both advantages and disadvantages. You can often get more in-depth answers from a non-structured interview and perhaps discover more about *why* and *how* things happen. On the other hand, the answers you get may be very difficult to analyse statistically. Some researchers begin with a few non-structured interviews that help them to identify what exactly they want to investigate. Then they move to a structured format and ask a larger number of people a simpler set of questions.

You can interview one person at a time, or talk to a group of people at once. Group interviews, which are also known as focus groups, are useful for investigating attitudes. The interaction between the people in the group can bring out more data than you might get in a one-to-one interview.

Interviewer: I'd be interested in hearing what you thought of the cover of the book.
A: It was all right.
B: Yes, it was quite attractive. Very bold.
C: I thought it was OK, but the colour was rather bright for my taste.
B: Shocking pink, that's what we used to call that colour.
A: I actually preferred the cover of the other book you showed us, the grey one. That was really nice.
Interviewer: Did anybody else like the grey colour better than the pink?

Experimental research

You are unlikely to commission a large research project without getting specialist advice, but it is interesting to know something about how experimental research is conducted. The first thing to do is to work out a hypothesis. This suggests a cause-and-effect relationship between two things you can measure, such as the temperature of a workshop and the speed at which a machinist works.

You would then set up an experiment in which you changed one variable (the temperature) and measured what happened to the other variable (speed of work). You could do your tests on the same group of machinists, over a period of time. Alternatively, you could test separate groups of machinists, working at different temperatures in otherwise identical circumstances.

You would need to show that any changes in work rates were unlikely to be caused by chance variations, or even the fact that the individuals concerned knew they were involved in an experiment and were working more quickly, or more slowly, as a consequence. To do this, you would have to set up a control group, where you tested the speed of work without changing the temperature.

ACTIVITY 27

What practical problems can you anticipate in arranging a study like this in a real workplace?

FEEDBACK

People might not want to co-operate with your experiment. It would probably not be covered by their contracts of employment. You might find it difficult to heat the workshop to a consistent temperature. Your experiment might interfere with normal production schedules. And there might be other circumstances, such as rush orders or interruptions, which interfered with your results.

If an experiment is to be truly scientific, everything else which could affect the results must be strictly controlled. The trouble with this is that you can't set up these laboratory conditions in a real workshop. On the other hand, if you put a machinist in a closed room where you can control the temperature and keep all other variables the same, you are setting up an artificial situation in which your subjects are unlikely to behave in a normal way. In many research projects, it is necessary to make a compromise between validity (how applicable the results are to the real world) and reliability (how you controlled your experimental conditions).

Networking

We will now take a look at some of the informal ways you can gather primary data. Networking is the name given to the practice of using a wide range of professional and personal contacts to obtain information. It cuts across organizational hierarchies and can give you access to facts and ideas that you would otherwise not have encountered. It is, of course, something that has been going on for centuries.

You know a lot of people reasonably well. These may be individuals you have encountered:

- at work – in your present organization, through your previous employment, through training courses and inter-organizational contacts, etc.
- because they are members of your family, or friends of family members through leisure activities
- from your time in education, at school, college or university

ACTIVITY 28

On a separate piece of paper, draw a map of the people you know. Put yourself in the middle and put different areas of your life on the spokes. Add extra forks where you need to. Write the names of the people you know on your map.

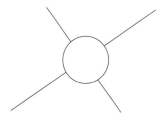

FEEDBACK

You probably found that there were at least sixty people on your network – maybe many more than this. All these people could be potential sources of information.

Let's suppose that you know sixty people reasonably well and that each of these individuals also knows about sixty people. And each of **these** people knows sixty people...

$60 \times 60 = 3600$

You are one handshake away from 3600 people.

$60 \times 60 \times 60 = 216\,000$

You are two handshakes away from 216 000 people.

$60 \times 60 \times 60 \times 60 = 12\,960\,000$

You are three handshakes away from 12 960 000 people.

In practice, things don't work out quite like this. Many of the individuals that the people on your network know will be the same as those you have listed yourself. Networks overlap. But on the other hand, many people have considerably more than sixty individuals on their network.

A few years ago, there was a party game in which players tried to work out how many handshakes they were away from a well-known personality, such as the Archbishop of Canterbury or one of the Kray twins. It was usually possible to establish a chain of three handshakes, or less, no matter who the target was. You can do the same thing if you are looking for people with expertise in a particular subject.

ACTIVITY 29

Choose one of these topics:

- fish-farming
- hot air balloons
- Indonesian cooking
- rave music

or choose another topic on which you really need information.

Does anyone on your network know about this topic? If not, can they point you towards someone who does?

FEEDBACK

If you take the trouble to do this activity, you will probably find someone who has knowledge of your topic.

However, there are dangers in relying too much on your network to provide information. One of these dangers can be described as the 'brother-in-law syndrome'. At some time or another, you have probably been into someone's house and seen an extraordinarily bad piece of decorating or building work. When you ask who is responsible, the owner of the house proudly says, 'Oh yes, my brother-in-law did that for me!' Just because you know someone, it doesn't mean that he or she is necessarily the best person to do a job. And just because you are introduced to someone who has a knowledge of fish-farming, it doesn't mean that this is the world expert on the subject.

Use your network to provide introductions to new areas of information. Useful questions to ask include:

- Where could I read about the latest research in this area?
- Which organizations are active in this field?
- What are the main trade journals?
- What are the key books?
- Who are the key people in this field?

You can then make contact with more formal, and verifiable, sources of information.

Another problem with using networks is that they cannot always be relied upon for timely information. You may not be able to wait until an ex-colleague has dinner with his squash partner next week and asks a crucial question on your behalf. For this reason, networking is often a more useful source of information in the early stages of an investigation, when you are not subject to time pressure.

If you take from your network, you must also give to it. This means that you must be prepared to provide information, advice and contacts when asked. If you don't co-operate in this way, sooner or later people will get fed up with helping you.

Networking on the Internet

Instead of relying on your own network, you can now link up with an international electronic network on the Internet. You can find newsgroups and forums where people with similar interests can exchange information. You can do this by posting a question:

I'm thinking about starting up a fish farm. Could anybody give me some advice on the sort of site I should be looking for?

If you put your question in the right place, you will almost certainly find someone who is willing to share his or her experience. You can then embark upon a useful correspondence. Sometimes, you can also join on-line conferences and discussion groups, which can give you an insight into new areas.

Sites on the Internet are frequently connected by hypertext links. If you are looking at a page dealing with university research into fish farming, you may be able to click on words or images that will take you to related sites belonging to different organizations.

ACTIVITY 30

If you have access to the Internet, try this experiment. Think up a specific question about the topic you investigated in Activity 29. Give yourself up to fifteen minutes to locate a site where you can get the information you need immediately – or post your question. If you leave a question, come back to the site twenty four and forty eight hours later and check your replies.

Then compare your success with the results of Activity 29. Which method yielded information that was more:

- relevant
- current
- adequate
- timely
- reliable
- cost-effective

FEEDBACK

There is a lot of useless information on the Internet. However, if you can develop the skills to find your away around, you should find it an invaluable source of timely and reliable data.

Complete your work in this section by doing the following activity.

ACTIVITY 31

1 Think of a topic on which you need to gather information

2 Make notes on how:

- relevant

- current

- adequate

- timely

- reliable

- cost-effective

you need this information to be

3   What kind of data do you need?

- Secondary data

- Primary data

- Qualitative data

- Quantitative data

4   What data source (or sources) will you use?

Why?

Look back at your answers to this activity at a later date, when you have gathered your information and made your decision. Assess the quality of the information and appropriateness of your sources.

Managing data and information

Now that you have used some data sources in your search for information, you are in a good position to think in more general terms about the way storage systems operate within your organization. If you prefer to move straight on to the decision-making process, read Section 3 next and come back to these pages later.

TO STORE OR NOT TO STORE?

Once you have taken a decision, you have to decide what to do with the data you gathered. Do you throw it away, or file it for future reference? If you will need the information to monitor the results of your decision, you obviously have to keep it. However, you may well have collected a lot of material that, although not strictly relevant to the decision itself, could well come in useful if you ever have to take a similar decision again.

The storage of information takes space, time and money. You have to balance this use of resources against the time and money it would take to find the information if you needed it again.

ACTIVITY 32   D4.1, D4.2

Look at the data you have collected for a decision you are taking at the moment, or have just taken. Ask yourself these questions:

■ When am I going to need this data again?

■ Will it still be current at that time?

■ What are the costs of storing it?

■ What are the costs of re-acquiring it?

■ Could anyone else in the organization use this data?

■ Is it already duplicated within the organization?

■ Is there a central site where I could make this data available?

Now decide what you will do with this data.

FEEDBACK

It is not always easy to balance the costs of keeping or re-acquiring data. You may not be comparing like with like. You may, for example, have to compare the financial cost of buying an obscure trade directory with the cost to your time (and temper) of having such a large collection of books that you cannot find a particular volume when you need it.

This activity asked you to consider other sites within your organization where data is held. Most people have access to several collections of data and information:

- your personal store of data and information
- data and information kept within your department or section
- data and information which is stored centrally

Some of these collections may duplicate each other unnecessarily. You may want to have your own copy of some internal documents on a temporary basis, while you are working on a particular project, but do not need to keep them permanently. However, it is important to keep the data and information you refer to most frequently within easy reach.

ACTIVITY 33

Go through your desk drawers and filing cabinet. Check the hard drive of your computer. Look at what you keep in your personal store of data and information.

Could you move any items to other sites within the organization?

Could you get rid of any items?

Is there anything that it would be useful to add to your personal store?

Compare your answers with these:

'I have my own copies of letters I have sent, although copies are also stored by the administrator of the department. It is not necessary to keep two sets.'

'I have a complete drawer of my filing cabinet full of early drafts of a major report I completed two years ago. Their time has come!'

'Every time I write a letter, I have to consult an address book. Since I write on a pc, I should keep a list of addresses I use regularly stored on the hard drive.'

RETRIEVING DATA

If you do decide to store data, you must be able to get hold of it again easily when you need it. If you don't, you might as well have thrown it away in the first place. There are two connected aspects to the storage and retrieval of data:

- you need a system in which you can place your data
- you need to identify your data

Storage systems can use various methods of classification. Paper-based records can be arranged:

- by subject
- alphabetically
- by frequency of use
- by date
- by reference number

Some records are even stored by size! The method of classification is related to the reason why the records are kept. Unless it is part of an organization-wide system, it may have been chosen by the person who has to use the system most regularly. It may, however, be completely impenetrable to other occasional users.

ACTIVITY 34

Examine the classification system used to store data and information in your department.

Is it related to an organization-wide system of classification?

Can you understand it?

Could all members of staff who might need to use the system understand it?

Think about the guides and signposts you used when searching other data sources. Could you use any of these to make your own data sources more accessible?

FEEDBACK

If you found difficulty in understanding the system, and it is independent of a larger classification system, consider changing it or introducing some method of indexing or cross-referral, so that it is possible to find data and information without the help of the individual who set up the system.

A good data storage system makes it easy to extract the information you need. It should also be consistent with the other systems in the organization, so that data can be linked. And it should also make the recording of data as simple and automatic as possible.

ELECTRONIC DATABASES

Data that is stored on an electronic database can be used much more flexibly. A database record is like a form, in which a box (called a field) can be indexed and searched. There are several types of field:

- a character (or alphanumeric) field contains words, such as names, streets, towns or codes
- a numeric field contains figures, such as amounts of money, which can be used for calculations
- a date field contains dates
- a logic field contains yes/no or true/false answers to questions such as 'Service agreement?'

You can instruct the database to show you any records in which, for example, the town field = Birmingham or the amount paid is greater than £200. This provides instant access to information. When a database is designed, it is essential that thought is given to the ways in which it will be used in future. As long as the appropriate fields are set up, the information they contain can be retrieved and analysed.

ACTIVITY 35

Look at the databases used in your department and discuss them with the people who enter data and extract information.

How easy is it to enter data?

How easy is it to extract information?

Could these databases yield more (or more useful) information than you are taking from them at the moment?

FEEDBACK

Some commercially designed databases are very sophisticated indeed. The specifications may be much higher than you actually need. This could mean that staff are entering unnecessary data. On the other hand, it could also mean that you could get much more information from them, if you used their facilities more fully.

IDENTIFYING DATA

Once you have an adequate system for storing data and information, you must make sure that items are properly identified within it. Common mistakes with paper-based storage systems include:

- forgetting to date items
- mixing up different drafts
- wrongly classifying items

Common mistakes with electronic databases include:

- putting things under the wrong field, such as the town under the postcode field
- writing numbers in a character field, where they won't be recognized as numbers
- duplicating records without realizing it

SECURITY

If you store data that contains personal details of individuals or information that is of a commercially sensitive nature, you must make sure that it is secure.

ACTIVITY 36

Do you use computers for any of the following purposes?

- processing accounts

- checking credit rating

- payroll and personnel data

- marketing and sales information

- word processing

- electronic mail

FEEDBACK

If you store data on computers for any of these purposes, you need to know about the Data Protection Act.

The Data Protection Act lays down rules about the handling of personal information, which is defined as:

personal information about identifiable living individuals held in automatically processed form

This can include details such as names, addresses, customer history and credit rating. The Data Protection Act is based around eight principles.

1   The information to be contained in personal data shall be obtained, and personal data shall be processed, fairly and lawfully.

2   Personal data shall be held only for one or more lawful purposes.

3   Personal data held for any purpose or purposes shall not be used or disclosed in any manner incompatible with that purpose or those purposes.

4   Personal data held for any purpose or purposes shall be adequate, relevant and not excessive in relation to that purpose or those purposes.

5   Personal data shall be accurate and, where necessary, kept up to date.

6   Personal data held for any purpose or purposes shall not be kept for longer than is necessary for that purpose or purposes.

7   An individual shall be entitled

   (a) at reasonable intervals and without undue delay or expense

      (i)   to be informed by any data user whether he holds personal data of which that individual is the subject; and

      (ii) to access to any such data held by the data user; and

   (b) where appropriate, to have such data corrected or erased

8   Appropriate security measures shall be taken against unauthorized access to, or alteration, disclosure or destruction of, personal data and against accidental loss or destruction of personal data.

ACTIVITY 37

Which principles of the Data Protection Act, if any, are relevant to the following activities?

1 Selling an electronic database listing the names and addresses of your customers to another organization.

2 Throwing a floppy disk containing personal details of employees onto a skip.

3 Using the results of an anonymous survey of people's spending habits to plan an advertising campaign.

4 Using out-of-date data to assess customers' credit rating.

FEEDBACK

1 This would be prohibited by the third principle, unless customers' permission was sought when they provided the data.

2 This could give unauthorized people access to the data and is forbidden by the eighth principle.

3 Since this data is anonymous, it is not covered by the Act, which only deals with information about identifiable living individuals.

4 The fifth principle states that data should be accurate and, where necessary, kept up to date.

ACTIVITY 38 D4.2

How much care goes into the storage of personal data in your department? What do you do to ensure that it is:

- adequate

- accurate

- not excessive

- up to date

- not accessible to unauthorized people

- only used for lawful purposes

- not altered or destroyed accidentally

FEEDBACK

If you have any concerns about the way personal data is stored on computer in your department, you must improve your procedures.

Summary

Now that you have finished this section you should be able to:

- describe the difference between data, information and knowledge
- gather quality information
- assess whether you need quantitative or qualitative information
- transform quantitative and qualitative data into information
- describe the advantages and disadvantages of primary and secondary data sources
- use primary and secondary data sources
- decide which data and information you should store
- assess data storage systems for accessibility and security

Section 3 Using information to make decisions

This section describes techniques you can use to make use of the information you have gathered to make decisions. It begins by focusing on some methods that can be used to find pattern and meaning in numbers.

You will be taken step-by-step through a process of rational decision making. This is a model that you can apply to any situation where you have to make a choice from a number of options. You will also look at other methods of making decisions and consider how you can use them most effectively. The section ends by looking at the risks associated with decisions, and what you can do to minimize them.

Making sense of figures

We'll begin this section by looking at some techniques you can use to organize quantitative data so that it can be used for decision making.

AVERAGES

Imagine that you want to know how long to allow for a particular part of a process. You check back in the records and find that, on the previous ten occasions it has been performed, the activity has taken the following numbers of days:

2, 4, 5, 3, 4, 4, 6, 10, 5, 4

As it stands, you can't do much with this data. You need to find an average figure that you can build into your schedule.

There are three ways of working out an average. The mean is obtained by adding up all the results and dividing the total by the number of results. In this example, you would get

$$\frac{47}{10} = 4.7 \text{ days}$$

The problem with this figure is that it is distorted by the one time that the activity took ten days. This was an untypical result that may have been caused by special circumstances, but it has affected the average figure.

The **median** is the middle result if you arrange all the results in order, like this:

2 3 4 4 4 4 5 5 6 10

Because there is an even number of results in this set, you actually have to take the two middle results and divide them by 2, to get a median of 4. The median is useful in situations where you have one or two extreme results.

Another way of looking at these results is to ask the question: 'How long does it usually take?' The **mode** is the result that occurs most frequently. In this set of numbers, 4 crops up more often than any of the other numbers, so 4 is the mode.

ACTIVITY 39

You are negotiating the renewal of a service contract for a piece of office equipment. The contractors say that they have been called in seven times over the last year, and the cost to them of making the repairs has been:

£30
£35
£35
£40
£40
£40
£180

They say that this averages out at £57.14 a visit, and therefore want to increase the cost of the contract next year.

What would you say to them?

FEEDBACK

You should point out to the contractors that they have worked out the mean, which has been distorted by one unusually large figure. If you can argue that a similar expense is unlikely to arise again, you should suggest that it would be fairer to look at the median or the mode, either of which would give an average cost of £40 per visit, and the new contract should be based on this figure.

GROUPING YOUR DATA

When you are looking at a large number of figures, it can be helpful to summarize them by putting them into groups. For example, imagine that you work in a large factory. You are planning some staff training and want to find out which type of people to direct it at first. You have a printout in front of you that lists the number of times last year each worker produced goods that were rejected by the quality checkers.

The printout starts like this...

Name	D.O.B.	Employed	Line	Faulty goods
Achen, J.	23.1.71	22.4.96	A	40
Alvarez, M.	5.7.65	30.5.94	B	20
Attwood, P.	3.9.50	19.3.85	B	63
Aziz, M.	4.6.48	9.11.89	E	21
Brown, T.	6.3.72	16.10.90	C	49

and continues for several pages, giving the same information for all 250 people who work on the assembly lines. It is impossible to draw any conclusions from this mass of data unless you organize it in some way.

One way you could organize this data would be to list people in order of the number of faulty goods they produced, and direct your training at the top section of the list first. However, there is a high staff turnover in your factory, and many of the worst offenders are no longer working for the company. You need to group people in some other way.

Another method you could use is to look at the records on the five different assembly lines. You would do this by taking everyone on Line A, and working out the mean number of mistakes per year, then doing the same for Lines B, C, D and E. You could then put the results on a bar chart as shown in Figure 3. This tells you at a glance that Line A makes more mistakes.

Or you could group workers in another way, by age. You would have to divide the workforce into convenient age ranges, say 21–25, 26–30, 31–35, 36–40, 41–45, 46–50, 51–55, 56–60 and 61–65 and work out the mean number of mistakes for people in each group. You could then draw a histogram as shown in Figure 4. This tells you that the 21–25 age group makes most mistakes.

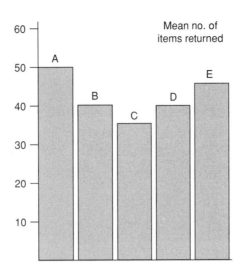

Figure 3   Bar chart showing mean number of mistakes by line

You may have noticed that the columns touch each other in the histogram, but have space between them in the bar chart. This is because the horizontal scale in a bar chart is used to define categories of items from different times or different places. The bars could be arranged in any order, and the graph would still have the same meaning. On a histogram, the sequence of numbers on the horizontal axis has some meaning. Here, it shows the increase in age of the workers. By the way, it is important that the intervals between the numbers on the horizontal axis are the same.

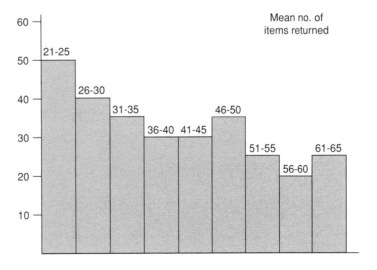

Figure 4   Histogram showing mean number of mistakes by age group

ACTIVITY 40

Look back at the printout. How else could you group the workers?

Would you present this information on a bar chart or a histogram?

FEEDBACK

The printout also gave the date at which each worker began his or her employment at the factory. This might be a better way of deciding which group needed training. The graph you would use to present the results would be a histogram, because it would have a numerical scale (showing years or months of employment) on the horizontal axis.

DISTRIBUTION

If you have a large number of figures, you often need to summarize them in some way. The mean, median or mode will give you three different types of average. The range, which is the difference between the lowest and highest figure, is also useful in some situations. However, freak results at the low and high ends of the scale can sometimes make the range somewhat misleading.

Although 75 per cent of the phone calls were made in less than two minutes, the shortest lasted only ten seconds and the longest 25 minutes.

Another statistic, the **standard deviation**, gives you information about how tightly the figures are clustered around the mean. Imagine that you have done a survey on the number of cups of coffee that members of staff buy from the office machine in a week. Your results are shown in Table 2.

Table 2 Cups of coffee bought each week

Cups of coffee	People
1	1
2	3
3	4
4	6
5	11
6	12
7	10
8	8
9	6
10	4
11	3
12	2
13	1
14	1

You can get a better impression of what is happening if you present the figures as shown in Table 3.

Table 3 Cups of coffee bought each week

Cups of coffee	People
1	●
2	●●●
3	●●●●
4	●●●●●●
5	●●●●●●●●●●●
6	●●●●●●●●●●●●
7	●●●●●●●●●●
8	●●●●●●●●
9	●●●●●●
10	●●●●
11	●●●
12	●●
13	●
14	●

Each dot represents one person who comes into this category. You can see that the dots form a sort of curve. The most popular number of cups of coffee is 6 – and the line curves down on each side to the least popular number. You often get a curved shape like this when you arrange data to show how frequently things happen.

Now imagine that you did a similar survey on people's tea-drinking habits, and produced the results shown in Table 4.

Table 4   Cups of tea bought each week

cups of tea	people
1	●
2	●●
3	●●
4	●●
5	●●●
6	●●●●
7	●●●
8	●●
9	●●
10	●
11	●
12	●
13	●
14	●

You can probably see that this curve is much flatter. The number of people in the most popular groups, where the frequency is highest, is not very different from the numbers in the groups at the edges of the curve. The standard deviation gives you a statistic that you can use to compare the shape of these two curves. It tells you the average amount by which all your results deviate from the mean.

You can work it out like this, although we don't necessarily recommend that you try it now:

1   Start by working out the mean for all the values. In the example of the cups of coffee, this would be the total number of cups bought, divided by the total number of people.

2   For each group, subtract the mean (which you worked out in step 1) from the value (the number of cups bought).

3   For each group, calculate the square of your results in step 2.

4   For each group, multiply this figure by the frequency (the number of people in the group).

5   Now add up the results you worked out in step 4 and divide this figure by the total frequency (the total number of people in the survey).

6   Finally, take the square root of this figure. You now have the standard deviation.

As you can imagine, working out the standard deviation on paper is a lengthy process. Luckily, computer programs exist which can do the calculations for you, even taking the figures directly from spreadsheets.

The larger the figure you have for the standard deviation, the more dispersed are your results.

ACTIVITY 41

Can you think of any situations in which it would be useful to know the standard deviation as well as the mean?

FEEDBACK

It is helpful to know the standard deviation in many situations where you are comparing different sets of data. Your example may be similar to this one:

'We were comparing the times it took to perform the same task using different systems. We had the average (mean) time for each system, but it was also important to know which system was more consistent. We chose the system which had the smaller standard deviation, even though the mean time was slightly greater.'

TRENDS

If you have data that has been collected over a period of time, you can arrange it to provide information about what is likely to happen in the future.

ACTIVITY 42

Look at Figure 5. What does it tell you about the past?

What do you think is likely to happen in 1997?

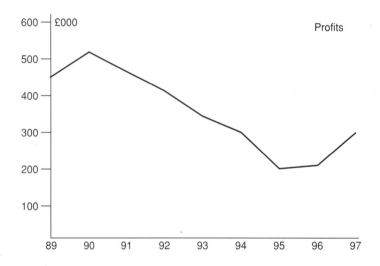

Figure 5   Graph for Activity 42

FEEDBACK

The graph tells you that profits more than halved in the years 1989 to 1995. At that point, the decline was halted and profits now appear to be going up again. You could not make any predictions for 1997 on the basis of this graph alone, because the upturn has only been going on for a year. It could be a temporary blip. However, the graph could indicate the type of questions you should be asking. Why did the profits decline before 1995? What was done in 1995 to remedy the situation? You could then assess whether the action taken was likely to be effective. If it is, then you could expect profits to continue to rise. If it is not going to be effective, then the long-term decline of the company will probably resume, and it may not stay in business much longer.

Sometimes you have data that varies a great deal from one period to the next. For example, if you were looking at the monthly sales figures of a shop that specialized in school uniforms, you would probably see peaks during the months that contained the start of a new term. If the line on a graph is zigzagging up and down, it can be difficult to see underlying trends. It is helpful to even out the peaks and troughs by working out what is known as the **moving average.** This is done by plotting another line on the graph that shows the mean results for a longer period, usually twelve months, which ended in the month in the question.

CORRELATION

You often need to know whether one activity or set of circumstances affects something else. If you put more people on the tills of a supermarket, do sales rise? Is there any relationship between the number of special offers that you advertise and the total level of sales? If you increase (or decrease) the volume of piped music, do people buy more? In order to answer these questions, you need to know the **correlation** between two things.

You can look for a correlation by drawing a scatter diagram, as shown in Figure 6.

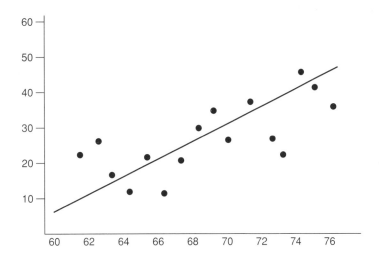

Figure 6   A scatter diagram

In this example, the horizontal axis shows the outside temperature in degrees Fahrenheit and the vertical axis shows the number of ice creams sold. Each dot represents an occasion when the temperature was measured and the number of ice creams was counted. A straight line has been drawn through the dots, with an equal number of dots each side of it. This shows clearly that the number of ice creams sold rises when the temperature goes up. This is known as a positive correlation: as one value goes up, so does the other value that you are measuring.

If you drew a scatter diagram showing how many hot drinks were sold from a stall when the temperature was at different levels, you would expect to see the straight line going in the other direction. This would be an example of a negative correlation: as one value goes up, the other falls.

As well as knowing which direction the line goes in, it is useful to know how tightly the dots are clustered around it. The closer they are to the line, the stronger the relationship between the two variables you are examining. The statistic that gives you this information is the **correlation coefficient**, which is usually represented by the letter r. The maths necessary to calculate the correlation coefficient is beyond the scope of this book, but you should be able to recognize the significance of this statistic when you see it.

- A correlation coefficient of −1 is a perfect negative coefficient
- A correlation coefficient of 0 indicates that there is no relationship between the two variables
- A correlation coefficient of +1 is a perfect positive coefficient

ACTIVITY 43

Which correlation coefficient is likely to belong to each of these situations?

(a) −0.1
(b) −0.8
(c) +0.7

1 The number of customer complaints received in relation to the amount spent on customer care spending.

2 The height of employees in relation to their success rate making telephone sales calls.

3 The months of experience workers have had and the speed with which they perform a particular activity.

You can use correlation coefficients to compare different sets of data. They can help you find out more about cause and effect and to predict the consequences of future actions.

PIE CHARTS

If you were told that a local authority took more than five working days to arrange care packages for clients on 2420 occasions in a single year, you might think it needed to re-examine its procedures as a matter of urgency. However, if you were shown a diagram such as Figure 7, you would be able to see this number in context.

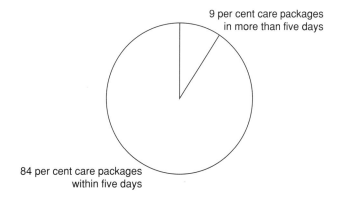

Figure 7 A pie chart

Pie charts allow you to see how the parts of a situation relate to the whole. They are useful for gaining a sense of perspective, particularly if you are dealing with large figures.

The rational decision-making model

This method of taking decisions was developed by Kepner and Tregoe in their book *The New Rational Manager*. It provides a framework that you can use for any decision where it is worth investing time and resources in identifying the best answer. There are twelve stages in the process:

1　Define the decision
2　Establish the objectives
3　Classify the objectives
4　Define the MUSTS
5　Define the WANTS
6　Generate the alternatives
7　Apply the alternatives to the requirements
8　Test the alternatives against the MUSTS
9　Score the remaining alternatives against the WANTS
10　Multiply the weights by the scores
11　Come to a provisional decision
12　Make a final decision

We'll look at each of these stages in turn.

1 Define the decision

Start by stating exactly what decision you are taking. This helps clarify your thinking and lets everyone involved know what the real issues are.

Some important clients from another part of the country are coming to an all-day meeting at your organization. You have to decide what to do with them at lunchtime. It's common practice in your organization to order a range of gourmet sandwiches to eat at the meeting table, but you don't think this solution is appropriate on this occasion. You realize that you need to impress these particular clients by taking them out to lunch. So the decision you have to take is: Where shall I take these clients out to lunch?

2 Establish the objectives

Next, consider what the perfect answer to your decision would achieve. You will probably have to gather some information to work out some objectives that are attainable and realistic. It doesn't matter if some of your objectives are incompatible at this stage. However, wherever you can, make them measurable.

ACTIVITY 44

Think of some suitable objectives for the decision about where to take important clients out to lunch.

FEEDBACK

Your objectives may be similar to these:

- price per person not over £30
- good wines available
- good food
- the clients will be impressed with the service and atmosphere
- local dishes served, to remind clients of their visit to this part of the country
- some degree of privacy, so we can talk business during the meal
- the meal will take less than an hour and half in total
- within five minutes' drive of the office

3 Classify the objectives

You now have to decide which of your objectives you absolutely must have – and which you would like to have, but can live without, if absolutely necessary. The difference between a MUST and a WANT is that if one of the options you consider doesn't meet a MUST objective, it should be rejected.

ACTIVITY 45

Sort out your own list of objectives into MUSTS and WANTS.

MUSTS	WANTS

FEEDBACK

The objectives given in the feedback to the last activity could be classified like this:

MUSTS	WANTS
■ good food	■ price per person not over £30
■ the clients will be impressed with the service and atmosphere	■ good wines available
■ some degree of privacy, so we can talk business during the meal	■ local dishes served, to remind clients of their visit to this part of the country
■ the meal will take less than an hour and a half in total	
■ within five minutes' drive of the office	

The way that you classify your objectives into MUSTS and WANTS will depend entirely on your priorities. It could be that the price of the lunch is a crucial factor, or that you would be prepared to take a little longer over the meal if you could find somewhere really special.

4 Define the MUSTS

Now look more closely at your MUSTS. Find a way of measuring them, or a standard that an option should meet in this area. For example, you might consider that a suitable standard for 'good food' was that the restaurant had a certain number of rosettes or stars in a restaurant guide. The reason for doing this is that you need some non-subjective (and relatively easy) way of telling whether an option meets these criteria.

5 Define the WANTS

Think about how important each of the WANTS is to you and give it a numerical weighting out of 10. Give 10 points for something that is really important, and less than 10 for something that is less significant.

This is how you might weight the WANTS in the feedback to the last activity:

- price per person not over £30 (10)
- good wines available (8)
- local dishes served, to remind clients of their visit to this part of the country (5)

Once again, the amount of weight you give to each point depends entirely on your own priorities.

6 Generate the alternatives

Now you have to assemble your list of options. This is an information-gathering exercise. Remember the advantages (and disadvantages) of collecting either primary or secondary data – and the characteristics of quality information.

ACTIVITY 46

Think of three ways in which you could gather information about local restaurants.

1

2

3

Your methods might have included some of these ideas:

- ask around the office
- drive around the area
- consult a restaurant guide
- look at advertisements in the local/national press
- phone around restaurants listed in the *Yellow Pages*

Once you've found out more about the options available, you may decide that you want to modify your MUSTS and WANTS. For example, if you discovered that one particular restaurant had panoramic views of the river, you might think about adding 'pleasant surroundings' to your list of WANTS. If this happens, adjust your MUSTS and WANTS before moving on.

7 Apply the alternatives to the requirements

Assemble the options in a format that makes it easy for you to compare them. If you relied on a restaurant guide for your information, you might do this by marking the relevant pages in the guide and writing a list of your options on a piece of paper:

- Riverbank Restaurant
- Wilsons
- Carabinos
- Le Trottoir

8 Test the alternatives against the MUSTS

Now go through your list of MUSTS and reject any options that don't meet all these criteria. For example, if you discovered that although Le Trottoir met all your other essential requirements, it was very noisy and crowded, it would have to be crossed off the list.

9 Score the remaining alternatives against the WANTS

You will now have a shorter list of options, all of which meet your essential requirements. The choice will now be made on how well they score against each of your WANT objectives. It helps to draw up a chart at this stage.

WANTS	WEIGHT	Riverbank	Wilsons	Carabinos
price	10			
good wines	8			
local dishes	5			
TOTAL				

Look at each WANT at a time. Give each of the options a score out of 10 for this feature. Give the alternative that best meets this WANT your top score, and score the other proportionately.

WANTS	WEIGHT	Riverbank	Wilsons	Carabinos
price	10	9	10	7
good wines	8	7	8	10
local dishes	5	10	8	5
TOTAL				

Notice that because Carabinos is the most expensive restaurant among the three, it receives the lowest score on price.

10 Multiply the weights by the scores

You must now fill in the empty columns on your table by multiplying the weights by the scores.

WANTS	WEIGHT	Riverbank		Wilsons		Carabinos	
price	10	9	90	10	100	7	70
good wines	8	7	56	8	64	10	80
local dishes	5	10	50	8	40	5	25
TOTAL							

11 Come to a provisional decision

Now add up the scores and see which option does best.

ACTIVITY 47

Which restaurant comes out on top?

FEEDBACK

You should have given the Riverbank Restaurant 90+56+50 = 196 points, Wilsons 100+64+40 = 204 points and Carabinos 70+80+25 = 175 points. So Wilsons is your first choice, closely followed by the Riverbank Restaurant.

12 Make a final decision

If you find that two or more options score similar totals, check that you are happy with the weightings and scores you gave earlier in the process. For example, if you decide that good wines are really not as important as you thought they were, you could find that the Riverbank Restaurant actually comes out on top.

THE ITERATIVE METHOD

You might decide that it was not worth going through the whole of the rational decision-making process to choose a restaurant. One quicker variation is to use the iterative process:

1 Work out a list of MUSTS
2 Pick an option and see if it meets these criteria
3 If it does, choose that option
4 If it doesn't, pick another option
4 Continue until you have found an option which meets all your criteria

This method will not guarantee that you make the *best* choice that is available, but it will allow you to make an acceptable choice in a short amount of time.

Decision trees

Sometimes you may have a complicated decision to make which involves thinking about the possible consequences of various courses of action. It can be very helpful to draw up a diagram that clarifies these alternatives.

A decision tree is built by using two types of fork.

Activity forks show points where a decision must be made.

Event forks show points where more than one outcome is possible.

At its simplest level, a decision tree is useful for examining the roles that choice (decisions) and chance (activity) play in a process. It gives you a map of what could happen. For example, the decision tree in Figure 8 shows what could happen if you asked for (or did not ask for) a full survey on a building you were considering buying in the hope of selling it to a particular buyer.

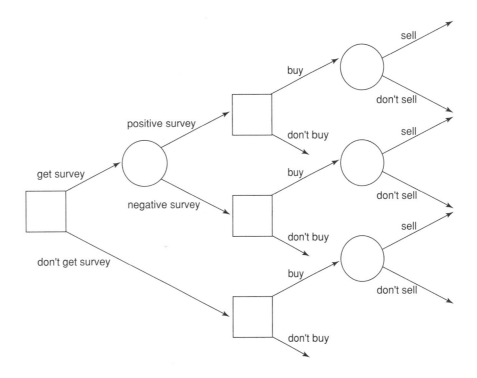

Figure 8   A decision tree

This diagram reminds you that the decision about whether to buy the building is separate from the decision about whether to get a survey. Regardless of whether you get a survey, you may still go on to buy the building (or not) and sell it to your client (or not). Notice that buy/don't buy is an Activity fork, because you have a choice at this point. Sell/don't sell is an event fork, because you are dependent on circumstances you can't control – the decision of the potential buyer.

Although it is beyond the scope of this book, you can also produce a much more sophisticated decision tree, in which you assess the probability of the outcomes at each event fork and assess the monetary value of each outcome, based on the cash this outcome would yield, multiplied by the probability of it happening. When you have taken away any costs involved, such as the survey fees and the cost of the building, and placed all this information on the tree, you can trace through the route that is most likely to produce the best outcome. For example, you would be able to calculate whether the increased likelihood of selling the building to your client if it had a positive survey was worth the added cost of paying for a survey.

ACTIVITY 48

Draw a simple decision tree, using activity and event forks, to describe a decision you will have to take in the near future.

Would it be possible to assess the probability of the various events?

❑ yes
❑ no
❑ with difficulty

Would it be possible to give a monetary value to the various outcomes?

❑ yes
❑ no
❑ with difficulty

It is often reasonably easy to work out the expected monetary value of various events, but less easy to assess their probability with any accuracy. Even without this information, a decision tree can be a good way of clarifying a complicated choice.

Models and simulations

Computer programs have made it very easy to see the effect of different figures on a calculation. This can be a great aid to decision making. For example, if a formula has been worked out which relates the cost of raw materials to the total production costs of manufacturing a product, it is a relatively simple matter to feed numbers into a computer spreadsheet and find out the effect of buying raw materials at different prices. The hard work goes into producing the formula in the first place.

There are many different kinds of computer models. Some are automated versions of techniques that previously had to be worked out on a calculator and painstakingly plotted on a graph. For example, it is now possible for someone without specialist mathematical knowledge to use linear programming to chart the constraints on a situation. Decision trees and critical path analysis diagrams can also be produced automatically.

Other types of model do not ask you to enter figures at all, but take their data from the way you answer questions. Yet others can simulate the behaviour of machines such as tube trains and aircraft from the way you handle the controls.

An expert system is a computer program that tries to emulate the way an expert in a particular subject would take a decision. The system receives data, either by asking questions or by some other form of monitoring, and processes this information to produce a decision. Expert systems are expensive to develop, and are not yet able to cope with the wide range of situations that a human expert could handle. They do, however, have a surprising range of uses. Read this case study.

The Convention on International Trade in Endangered Species (CITES) prohibits the trade in plants and animals that are near to extinction. Customs and Excise officers are empowered to confiscate souvenirs made from endangered species. However, few customs officers are trained naturalists. It is also very difficult to tell whether a snakeskin purse or belt has been made from an endangered species of snake, or one on which there are no restrictions.

In order to solve this problem, a system known as NEMESIS has been developed. In order to check an item made of snakeskin, the customs officer focuses a special camera on it. The picture is processed by a computer and the pattern and shape of the scales, and other details, are analysed. All the customs officer has to do is click the mouse two or three times. A few seconds later, the computer produces a report that identifies the snake, says whether a special import licence is required and, if appropriate, quotes the relevant section and paragraph of the CITES agreement.

So far, the system can only analyse snakeskin, but it is hoped to develop it in other areas in the future.

ACTIVITY 49

This case study illustrates some of the advantages of an expert system. What do you think they are?

FEEDBACK

The system can be operated by someone without specialist knowledge of the subject. It is quick and easy to operate and can be used in a situation where a fast decision is necessary. It also produces authoritative information to back up its decision.

Computer models are capable of astonishing things. They can make faster (and usually more accurate) decisions than people. Although a model is expensive to develop, once it is up and running it is much cheaper to use than a human being with the same degree of skill and experience. However, a model is only a representation of reality. It cannot, unless told to do so, take into account all the factors that human beings are aware of.

Think back to the choice of restaurant made by the rational decision-making model earlier in the section. If you were using this method to make a decision, you could change the weighting you gave to your various criteria. You could turn a MUST into a WANT, or add other WANTS to your list. In other words, you could tinker about with the formula until it came up with an answer that you were happy with. This fine tuning would enhance the use of the model, not invalidate it. However, if the model was computerized, you would not be able to do this. In the first place, you probably would not understand the formula. And in the second place, the answer produced by the computer program would have a certain authority, which you might feel nervous about challenging. Both these problems are significant. Computer models allow people to take decisions that they would not be able to take unaided. Since people have to rely on the model, it can take on a mysterious, almost magical status. It becomes a 'black box'. This is the same thing that can happen to junior staff who do everything 'by the book'. They have become afraid to use their common sense. The answer is not to abandon computerized models, but to keep your faculties about you. Find out the principles that a computer model uses and be aware of when they do not coincide with your own perception of reality. At this point, what has been an 'off-the-peg' decision becomes a 'tailor-made' decision. You may be able to work out the answer yourself, but if you can't, seek help from someone with the necessary knowledge and experience.

Non-computer-based models

You can also test out some decisions in other ways, which have nothing to do with computers. For example, if you design a questionnaire, you should pilot it with a small group of people before you begin your full-scale survey. This will allow you to check whether you made the right decisions about:

- the number of questions
- how you phrased the questions
- the layout of the page
- the method you chose to analyse the results

ACTIVITY 50

What form of simulation would be helpful to test out these decisions?

■ a decision to invest in purchasing a videophone link

■ a decision to promote a member of your department

■ a decision to put a rhubarb-flavoured ice lolly onto the market

FEEDBACK

You could rent the videophone link system and assess its benefits before committing yourself to purchasing it. You could send this individual on a management course where he or she would be observed in situations requiring the exercise of new types of responsibility. You could test the rhubarb-flavoured ice lolly by asking a suitably chosen tasting panel to give their verdict.

These tests all have two things in common:

■ they require less resources than putting actual decision into action – and therefore involve less risk
■ they provide a lot of feedback

ACTIVITY 51

Now think of a decision you have to make in the near future. Are there any aspects of this decision that you could try out in a rehearsal, pilot or other type of simulation?

If so, what resources would this require?

What feedback would you get?

FEEDBACK

One way to assess whether a test or simulation is worth doing is to draw a decision tree. If the feedback you get reduces the risks you take when you make the real decision, it may well be worth the resources you put into it.

Group decision making

There are three main ways in which a group can arrive at a decision:

- debating
- discussion
- negotiation

DEBATING

This is the most formal way of coming to a decision. It's the method that is used in Parliament and also sometimes in board meetings, or meetings of governing bodies. The issue to be debated is expressed as a 'motion', such as:

This Board agrees to institute a no-smoking policy on company premises.

Somebody must 'propose' (speak in favour of) the motion. Sometimes, the motion will be seconded by someone else. Other people speak against it. It is usually possible to vary the wording of a motion, by putting forward an amendment:

This Board agrees to institute a no-smoking policy on company premises, apart from in a specially designated office in the basement.

The amendments are voted on first, and then the motion is voted for in its final form.

If you are involved in a formal debate, the most important thing you must do is to be absolutely clear about the standing orders, the rules by which the debate is run. These differ from organization to organization, and will be followed rigorously. For example, it may not be possible to table an amendment without giving notice beforehand, or to speak unless you are invited to do so by the chairperson.

In a debate, it is usual for speakers to declare their support, or lack of support, for the motion. This can make it difficult for uncertainties to be explored. If voting is not private, people feel constrained about which side they are seen to support. And the formality of a debate can make unconfident speakers, who may have valid points to say, unwilling to contribute.

DISCUSSION

This is the most common method of group decision making. It is less formal than a debate, and the issue can be looked at from many different angles. In a discussion, everyone is encouraged to have their say. This can be helpful in the early stages of making a decision, when it is important to consider the criteria and gather a wide range of options to choose from. One technique that is often used to generate ideas is brainstorming. Here, everyone is encouraged to contribute points that are recorded without criticism or comment. Afterwards, these points are grouped and analysed.

ACTIVITY 52

You are probably aware that group discussions are not always a satisfactory way of making decisions. What problems have you experienced?

FEEDBACK

- ■ Your answer may well include some of these points:
- ■ Discussion can be very time-consuming
- ■ People wander off the point
- ■ People are unwilling to change their point of view
- ■ Some people are unwilling to say what they think in an open discussion
- ■ The Chair may not be able to keep the discussion under control
- ■ There is often no satisfactory way of bringing a discussion to a close

Many of these problems can be alleviated if a discussion has a slightly more formal structure. Ground rules about when people can speak, and for how long, can help. It is useful to have a clear agenda with definite periods of time allowed for each stage of the discussion. The agenda can also state objectives for the discussion – to reach agreement on a certain issue.

Negotiation

In this situation, the parties have different – and often opposing – objectives for the decision. The aim of negotiation should be to reach an agreement that everyone can accept. If either side loses out completely, or discussions are abandoned because nobody will compromise, the negotiations have failed. The best result is a WIN-WIN situation, in which both sides achieve at least some of their objectives. The way to get to this conclusion is to move away from areas of confrontation and look for common ground.

Risk analysis

In ordinary life, people have a tendency to over-estimate the possibility of unlikely things happening – especially if these things coincide with their personal hopes or fears. This is why millions of lottery tickets are sold every week and why many older people are frightened to go out alone at night. At the same time, many of us have a tendency to under-estimate the risks of much more likely events – especially if we don't want them to happen or they reveal some unpleasant truth about ourselves.

ACTIVITY 53

Complete the sentence below in the way that seems appropriate to you.

'I know I've been unlucky with.................................in the past, but this time it's different.'

Have you ever said anything like this when warned of the risks of something you were about to embark on?

FEEDBACK

If you could identify with this statement, you are probably sometimes unwilling to acknowledge the risks associated with your decisions.

In management decision making, you need to get a realistic picture of the risks involved. Your first source of information here is what has happened in the past. For example, if you were considering using a supplier, you could assess:

- your organization's previous experience with this supplier
- other organizations' experience with this supplier
- the standing of this supplier within the industry, as demonstrated by its membership of trade associations or regulatory bodies

What happened in the past cannot guarantee what will happen in the future, but it will give you some *indication* of what is likely to happen. The further a decision takes you into unfamiliar territory, the riskier it is. For example, it is very risky to sell a new product in a new market, but less risky to sell a new product in an established market, or an established product in a new market.

Sometimes it is enough to make a subjective assessment of the risks. In other situations, you will need to quantify these dangers. It may be advisable to consult someone with an understanding of statistical probability. For example, if you were making decisions about a survey you were about to commission, a statistician would be able to tell you how representative of the general population the results would be if you sent questionnaires to 50, 100 or 500 people.

If a decision has important financial implications, you may need to prepare a sensitivity analysis. This describes the amount by which key figures, such as the cost of materials or labour, would have to change to turn a good investment into a bad one.

MINIMIZING RISK

There are two types of risk to consider:

■ the risk that something will prevent you implementing your decision
■ the risk that your decision will not produce the effects you expect

ACTIVITY 54

You have just taken a decision to book a particular hotel for a conference.

1   What could prevent you implementing the decision?

What could you do to reduce this risk?

2   Why might your decision not produce the effects you expect?

What could you do to reduce this risk?

FEEDBACK

1   Two problems you might encounter are that the hotel cannot take your booking or that the funds to pay for the conference are no longer available. You could protect yourself against these risks by checking the availability of these resources immediately before taking the decision and also, once the decision is made, confirming it as quickly as possible. You could also have a second choice of hotel ready, in case the first was not available.

2   The main risk you face here is that the conference facilities are not of the standard you expected. It is also possible that your original objectives were unrealistic, or that you chose the wrong selection criteria. You can minimize these risks by taking extra care with the first stages of a decision and ensuring that your information is accurate, adequate and current.

The key points to remember are:

■   get quality information on which to base your decision
■   be rigorous with your decision-making process
■   have a contingency plan
■   don't introduce further risks by delaying the implementation of your decision

Summary

Now that you have completed this section you should be able to:

■   use a variety of simple statistical and graphical techniques to organize quantitative data for decision making
■   use the rational decision-making model
■   draw up a simple decision tree
■   describe the use of models and simulations for decision making
■   use group decision-making techniques effectively
■   minimize the risk involved in decision making

Section 4 Decision making and communication

In this final section of the book we explore some of the communication skills associated with decisions. The section begins by considering how best to present a decision to other people so that they are clear about the options available to them.

You will also look at ways in which you can provide guidance to staff who have to make routine decisions. When you do this effectively, you will find that your own workload is lighter, because you have to intervene less frequently to explain or to put things right.

The next part of the section deals with the communication skills you need when announcing decisions to the people who will be affected by them. If you handle this part of the process well, your decisions are much more likely to gain acceptance.

Finally, you will be asked to consider how you will get feedback on your decisions. This will help you to monitor their effectiveness, and also to evaluate and develop your skill as a decision maker.

Communicating with decision makers

You will often be asked to do the groundwork on a decision which other people are actually going to take. This may involve:

- drawing up a list of options
- exploring the pros and cons of various alternatives, and
- making a recommendation

Alternatively, you may just be asked to gather evidence to support a particular option. In either situation, you need to present the facts as clearly and succinctly as possible to the decision makers.

Remember that the reason why you have been asked to do the preparatory work on the decision is to save other people's time. They do not want to know everything that you have found in the course of your investigations. Decision makers want knowledge, backed up by information. They do not want to have to analyse the data themselves. Use graphs and charts to organize what you have found out.

All they want to know is information that is of direct relevance to the decision. This usually means:

- the criteria on which the decision should be taken
- a list of options
- concrete details of what these options will involve
- a logical argument comparing the various options
- a recommendation
- warning of any risks associated with the chosen option

It is often possible to summarize most of this information on a chart. You have probably seen tables such as Table 5 in consumer magazines.

Table 5   Summary of information

Magazine racks	BEST BUY		
	Acme Star	Tokyo 339	Bologna Princessa
Capacity (no. of mags)	12	10	8
Styling	*	**	***
Price	24.99	29.99	45.99
Weight	1 kg	0.5 kg	1.5 kg
Height	30 cm	30 cm	35 cm
Width	50 cm	55 cm	60 cm
Depth	12 cm	15 cm	10 cm
Wall-mounted	✓	✗	✓
Durability	***	**	*
Assembly instructions	**	***	*

OUR VERDICT: The Acme Star is not pretty, but it makes up for its unexciting appearance with its strong construction, large capacity and attractive price.

This tells the prospective buyer a great deal of information to help him or her choose from these three products. Notice that the chart:

- contains precise data (such as the dimensions)
- uses ✓ and ✗ to indicate the presence or absence of a feature
- rates some features using a star system

The verdict at the bottom sums up the information, makes a recommendation and warns prospective purchasers of the Acme Star's main disadvantage – its looks.

You can use charts that follow the same principles as this one to sum up the different options in many different kinds of decision.

ACTIVITY 55   D4.1, D4.3

Use this framework to prepare a chart comparing three options for a decision you have made yourself recently. Don't worry about filling in the details in each cell of the chart. Concentrate on the criteria you list down the left-hand side and the method or methods you will use to give relevant information (✓ and ✗, star system, precise data, or some other way).

Show your chart to someone else and ask whether they think it would help them to make the decision.

Is there anything else they would want to know?

Do they feel that this presentation trivializes the decision?

FEEDBACK

There are obviously some types of decision where this kind of presentation is not appropriate. These could include situations where the criteria concern ethical matters or are sensitive or contentious in some other way. However, where practical decisions are to be taken, a chart of this kind can be extremely effective.

A chart may not give the decision makers all the information they need.

ACTIVITY 56

Imagine that you are in the position of having several hundred thousand pounds that you are about to invest in purchasing magazine racks. Look back at the chart. What other information might you want before making your decision?

FEEDBACK

You would probably want to see the three products in the flesh – or at the very least have high quality colour photographs in front of you.

You might also want to ask:

■ why these three products were selected for comparison?
■ why the criteria were selected?
■ on what basis the products were rated against the criteria for styling and durability – in other words, what tests were done?

You would probably also want some more details about:

■ reliability of supply
■ any other risks associated with the decision
■ any legal or financial implications

Depending on the significance of the decision, you will have to give a greater or lesser amount of background information. If you are writing a report comparing different options, much of this information can be put in the appendices. This allows you to keep your argument and recommendations clear and uncluttered, but lets the decision makers check on any data they want to be sure of. For example, if you were writing a report comparing the magazine racks, you would mention in the main text that you had subjected the three products to laboratory tests for strength of construction and summarize your results. Bar charts could be a helpful way to present these results. In the appendix, you could describe these tests in more detail.

ACTIVITY 57

Here is the framework for a report that has been prepared to help decision makers assess several options. Where would you put the:

- knowledge
- information
- data

Title page

Executive summary
a quick synopsis

Introduction
terms of reference and methodology

Main report

Conclusions and recommendations

Acknowledgements

References

Glossary

Appendices

FEEDBACK

Knowledge belongs in the summary, main report and the conclusions and recommendations. It will also be evident in the introduction, where you outline your methodology.

Information belongs in the main report.

Data belongs in the appendices and also in the glossary.

It is important that decision makers know the risks they are taking. If you don't tell them, you may come in for criticism if something goes wrong later on. There is no need to cause alarm by thinking up a list of all the possible disasters that could be associated with the various options. Be sensible and realistic, but if you do have any reasonable doubts, pass them on. Always back up what you say with facts and figures.

Company A is a well-established business, with over twenty branches throughout the UK and a turnover in excess of £9.5 million. Company B is a much smaller and newer organization. Although several of its products have won international design awards, our contract would be the first major order that it has handled.

Decision makers always want to know what will happen next, once they have made their decision. You must be ready with concrete details of procedures, schedules and other arrangements. Only include this information in your report if it is relevant to the decision itself.

Sometimes, you may have to persuade decision makers that they have to take a decision. They may not be aware that they have a problem, or that there is an opportunity that they can exploit. In this situation, you can use the following format:

- **Position**   Tell them what is happening at the moment
- **Problem**   Tell them about the problem or opportunity
- **Possibilities**   Discuss the options
- **Proposal**   Make your recommendation

Don't forget that in evaluating proposals, decision makers need to know some quite basic things, which are all too easily omitted. They are:

- What do you propose to do?
- What are the benefits?
- When are you going to do it?
- How much will it cost?

So far, we have concentrated on situations where you are asked to make an objective comparison of several options. This is not always the case. You may be asked to prepare a proposal promoting a particular option. Here, you don't have to tell the decision makers about all the disadvantages of the option you want them to take. You must, however, have thought about these potential problems and be ready to suggest solutions if somebody else brings them up.

You often have to make a difficult judgement here. If you are pretty certain that someone is going to see a particular feature of your option as a major disadvantage, then you should face it head on and, if you can, explain why this isn't the case. On the other hand, if you think that no one is going to notice a potential difficulty, you may decide not to draw people's attention to it. *Caveat emptor* – let the buyer beware. If you keep quiet, you must be sure that you are not breaking any legal requirements or falling short of your organization's ethical standards.

Occasionally, you may find that the option you are promoting simply doesn't match up to the specifications that the client requires. If this is the case, it is usually best to admit it and retire gracefully. If you don't, you will be letting yourself in for a lot of trouble if your option is chosen. By being open about the fact that your option is not viable in the present circumstances, you may lose out in the short term, but the client's respect for your fairness and integrity will rise immeasurably. When a suitable opportunity arises, the client is very likely to contact you again.

Setting up systems for off-the-peg decisions

In the first section of the book we looked at the difference between tailor-made and off-the-peg decisions. A tailor-made decision is one in which you make a full comparison between the various options, using techniques such as those described in Section 3. An off-the-peg decision is one where you go for a quick, ready-made answer. We will now consider some ways in which you can provide those answers, so that other people can take routine decisions on your behalf.

One approach is to tell people the underlying principles or rules they should remember when making the decision:

- Non-members are not allowed in the Members' Lounge
- Never leave a delivery on the doorstep. It can be stolen and may compromise household security
- 'Flexibility, quality and reliability'
- The management cannot be held responsible for damage to customers' belongings which are left on the premises
- Our mission is to provide customer care of the highest standard
- No admission after 4 pm

There is a mixture of different statements in this list. Some express the mission or the policy of the organization. Others describe regulations or security procedures. The thing that they all have in common is that they all need to be *interpreted* by the person who is taking the decision.

Let's look at one of the mission statements. Suppose that:

Our mission is to provide customer care of the highest standard

is printed on the letterhead of a builders' merchant. A customer telephones during the lunch hour, when all the senior staff are off the premises, and asks a junior sales assistant to arrange the immediate free delivery of one bag of sand. What is the assistant to do? The request seems unreasonable to the assistant, but the mission statement suggests that he should agree to it. He obviously needs more detailed guidance than this.

Another of the statements seems to offer more help to the person who has to take a decision:

Never leave a delivery on the doorstep. It can be stolen and may compromise household security

But does this mean that it's all right to leave a delivery in the front garden, as long as it can't be seen from the road? And what is the delivery person supposed to do if nobody answers the door?

The less experience the people who are taking routine decisions have, the more guidance you need to give them. It is sometimes necessary to give step-by-step instructions. Here is a set of instructions that a company gave to people it employed on a casual basis to deliver directories to household addresses:

> **Never leave a directory in a place where it can be seen from the road or by someone approaching the house.**
>
> Try to hand the directory to the householder and get a signature on your white form.
>
> If this is not possible, leave it with a neighbour and get a signature on your white form.
>
> If this is not possible, find a dry, safe place to hide the directory, such as in a porch or shed, and put a pink slip through the door saying where you have hidden the directory. Initial the white form yourself.
>
> If this is not possible, put a pre-printed blue slip through the door, asking the householder to telephone the office to arrange a time when he/she will be in to accept delivery of the directory. Write X on the white form.

This leaves very little room for doubt.

FLOWCHARTS

When a sequence of decisions has to be taken, it can be helpful to draw up a flowchart as shown in Figure 9.

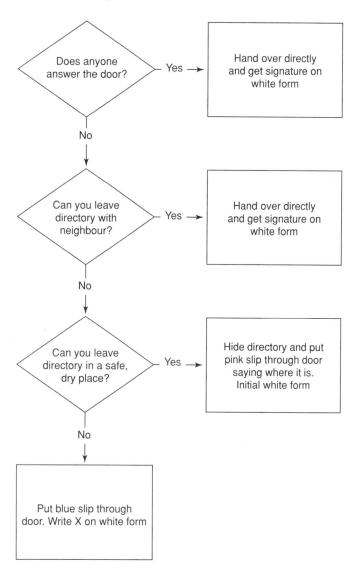

Figure 9   A flow chart example

ACTIVITY 58

Prepare a flowchart giving instructions to a sales assistant who has to decide whether or not to agree to deliver goods to a customer free of charge.

FEEDBACK

You should have put the criteria that are used to make the decision (such as cost of goods, weight of goods, status of customer, address to be delivered to) in the diamond-shaped boxes. The action to be taken (agree, don't agree, refer to manager) should have gone in rectangular boxes.

CHECKLISTS

Another way to clarify decisions is to prepare a checklist. This is a useful format if there are a lot of things that must be verified before a decision can be taken.

Check these points before passing an invoice for payment:

- ❑ Name of payee matches purchase order
- ❑ Amount matches purchase order
- ❑ Work description matches purchase order
- ❑ Signature of budget-holder present
- ❑ Invoice is coded
- ❑ Invoice is dated

ACTIVITY 59

Prepare a checklist that will help people in your department to decide whether a piece of work is acceptable. (Think of something that they have to make judgements about on a fairly regular basis.)

FEEDBACK

The content of your checklist will obviously depend on the type of work you were thinking of. Check the points you listed and make sure that it's absolutely clear whether you are saying that this feature ought to be present or ought *not* to be present in the work people are assessing.

You may have been slightly uncertain about how much to put in your checklist. You must cover all the important points, but should not insult people by stating the obvious, or take up their time unnecessarily. A good checklist is a helpful *aide-mémoire*, not an irritation.

Telling people about your decisions

When you have made a decision, you have to tell the people who will be affected by it. If the decision is good news, you will not find this difficult to do. However, if your listeners will not welcome your decision, you need to give some more thought to how you will communicate it.

Give the decision and explain briefly why it was necessary to take it. Use clear, direct language so that there can be no doubt at all about what you are saying. Do not get into a discussion about the decision itself. If people think that they can persuade you to change your mind, they will try to do it. If you are announcing a decision made by a senior colleague in the organization, you must act as though you support it, even if you don't personally agree with it. It is unprofessional to show your doubts in a situation like this, and will not help the people who are affected.

As the bearer of bad news, don't be surprised if you receive an unpleasant or even aggressive reaction. People can behave uncharacteristically if they are shocked, disappointed or concerned about their own future. They may attack you verbally, but try not to take this personally.

Think about when and where you will announce the decision. If it will have a particular impact on one member of staff, tell him or her privately. If it affects a whole group in a similar way, tell them together. If a department will be affected in different ways, try to tell the winners and losers separately, so they can express their elation or disappointment properly.

Always try to look forwards, not backwards. As soon as you can, get people to focus on the future. If the decision has very serious consequences, people may need a little time to absorb it before they are ready to think through the implications. When they are ready, allow an opportunity for them to ask all the questions they need to ask – and be ready with the answers.

Sometimes you need to sell a decision to the people who will be affected by it. You need to persuade them that what appears to be an unwelcome and problematic change is in fact an exciting opportunity. It is obviously both futile and patronizing to try this tactic in a situation where the decision really is bad news, such as redundancy or closure. However, there are many situations that can be viewed from more than one perspective. Try to get people to imagine what it will be like for them when the decision comes into force.

I had to tell another department that they were amalgamating with my own department. I knew that they would be very concerned about the future, as there had been a lot of rivalry between the two departments in the past. As soon as possible, I arranged a buffet lunch in the office, so that the two sets of people could begin to get to know each other. It was important that they began to think of each other as individuals, not 'that lot down the corridor'.

ACTIVITY 60

If you were announcing the relocation of your company to a new building twenty miles away, what could you do to help people imagine what the future will be like?

You could:

- take staff on a visit to the new building
- show them floor plans of the new offices and ask them to participate in planning their new workspace
- draw attention to any benefits of the new site, such as parking spaces and local leisure or shopping facilities
- reassure them about travel arrangements

SHOWING YOUR HAND

In many situations, people know that a decision is about to be made. If they have put in a proposal, applied for promotion or helped in negotiations with another organization, they will be waiting to hear the outcome. However, some decisions can come as a complete surprise to the people affected. You have to consider whether or not to warn them of what may happen.

On the first day of term, the Principal called all the lecturers together and said that there were going to have to be some cuts at the end of the academic year. They had to make savings of about £150 000 and this meant that one department, or section of a department, would have to go. They hadn't decided which department this would be, but would let us know as soon as possible. I suppose they told us to soften us up, so that the news wouldn't be such a shock when it came. Everyone felt pretty devastated. We all assumed it would be our own department, and started thinking about early retirement or finding another job. All enthusiasm about the term ahead went out the window.

In this situation, the effects of warning staff about the impending decision were entirely negative. The lecturers felt that there was nothing they could do to affect the decision and that they were only being told to weaken their resistance when the blow finally fell.

ACTIVITY 61

Can you think of any situations in which you should tell staff about an impending decision that will affect them?

The four main reasons for telling people about an impending decision are:

■   if they can contribute towards the decision-making process, either by supplying information or advising on the criteria that should be used

'I had to decide whether to ask our in-house graphic designers to do a particular job or put it out to freelancers. It was impossible to make this decision without discussing the matter with the Head of Design. I asked her to work out the costs of completing the job in-house.'

■   if they can contribute positively to the situation that makes the decision necessary

'I knew that we would have to make redundancies if we didn't reduce our costs. I spoke to the workforce and explained the situation. I put forward some definite ideas on how they could alter their work habits to save the organization money. Because they appreciated the seriousness of the situation, they were ready to comply with my instructions.'

■   if there are legal reasons to keep them informed

'I was considering dismissing an employee who had been off-hand with customers on more than one occasion. I had to follow the organization's disciplinary procedure and discuss the situation with the person concerned, giving him a formal warning. If I hadn't done this, we could have been sued for wrongful dismissal.'

■   if there are ethical reasons to keep them informed

'I knew that one of my most valued colleagues was considering taking on a big mortgage on a house that needed a lot of repair work. I also knew that senior management were seriously considering relocating to another area of the country. This was very difficult, because the information about the possible relocation was confidential, but I knew that if my colleague took on the mortgage and the firm decided to relocate, he would be in an impossible situation. I spoke to my own manager about the problem. In the circumstances, he agreed to bring forward the announcement that senior management were thinking about relocation.'

You can't always warn people of decisions that will affect them. There may be commercial reasons why you have to remain silent. Or you may consider that the damage done to the general morale outweighs any advantages to individuals or the organization. Telling people that you are about to take a decision also allows them to mount a campaign to influence the outcome.

ACTIVITY 62 D4.4

Think of a decision you will have to make soon that will affect other people.

List the reasons for and against discussing the decision **before** you take it with the people who will be affected by it.

For   **Against**

Will you tell them about the decision in advance? How will you tell them?

FEEDBACK

Make sure that the benefits that will arise from discussing (or not discussing) the decision in advance really outweigh the disadvantages.

Getting feedback on your decisions

You need to know whether a decision is having the desired effect. This means that you must have communication systems that will allow you to check on the quality of your decisions. If your decision is related to an ongoing process, these channels are probably set up already:

I have to make decisions all the time about which magazines we use to advertise our products. We code our coupons and ask anyone who telephones us where they heard of the organization. This allows me to monitor my decisions.

I monitor sales on a daily basis and know whether our buyers have made the right decisions.

I can tell from the level of production whether good decisions are being made at an operational level.

ACTIVITY 63

What systems do you use to check on decisions relating to ongoing processes?

FEEDBACK

The decisions you take in relation to an ongoing process are intended to keep it on track. You have a lot of information available about what *should* happen and can have systems in place that will alert you automatically if things begin to go differently.

If you are taking one-off decisions, it is more difficult to evaluate their quality. You have to compare what is *actually* happening (or has happened) with what you *expected* to happen. You need to have some way in which you can review the results of your decision. This could be:

- a probationary period for a new employee
- a system of performance review
- progress reports on a project
- debriefing sessions after a project is over

Finally, we will consider what we can learn from a decision that does not have the expected results:

Three months ago, you appointed a new deputy. You realized that you needed someone who could take responsibility for some of your day-to-day work and prepared a job description which reflected this role. You drew up a list of criteria for assessing applicants, which you used to evaluate the people who applied. You selected someone who met all the important criteria and gave him the job. You have tried to delegate some of your work to your new deputy, but he has made a mess of everything he has touched.

ACTIVITY 64

If this happened to you, what questions should you ask about the way you took your decision?

FEEDBACK

Something has clearly gone badly wrong here. It could have happened at any stage of the process. You must question:

- your original objectives – were they realistic?
- your choice of criteria – were they appropriate?
- the options that were available – did suitable candidates apply?
- the accuracy of the data you received – did the candidate mislead you?
- the adequacy of the data you received – did you ask the right questions?
- how you interpreted this data – should you have been more rigorous when you examined the applications?
- the conclusions you drew from your analysis of the information – did you apply your method of analysis properly?
- your method of analysis – was it a good way of comparing the candidates?

You must also consider whether something has changed in the environment that has a bearing on your decision and the way you made it. For example, if the nature of your own work has changed significantly in the last months, the qualities it requires will not have been reflected in the job specification that you drew up and it is not surprising that your new deputy cannot cope.

ACTIVITY 65   D4.3

Now think about a one-off decision that you made in the past and which did not
have the effects you expected. Try to identify why this happened. Was it because:

- something changed in the environment
- you had unrealistic objectives
- you set the wrong criteria
- you did not have an adequate range of options available
- you received inaccurate or inadequate data
- you processed this data wrongly
- you analysed your information wrongly
- you chose the wrong method to analyse your information
- something else? If so, what?

What did this experience tell you that will help you take better decisions in the
future?

FEEDBACK

The way in which you answered this activity is a good indication of how much you have learned from
working through this book. Hopefully, you will now have confidence in some aspects of your
decision-making technique and also feel able to make improvements to some other aspects. If you
were completely happy with the way that you took the decision and felt that it went wrong because
of a change in the environment, think back to the issues that were discussed in the first section of the
book. Perhaps you mistook a problem for a decision, or took a decision at the wrong time.

Summary

Now that you have completed this section you should be able to:

- use appropriate methods to present information to decision makers
- provide effective guidance to people taking routine decisions
- inform people of your decisions
- obtain feedback on your decisions
- assess your own competence as a decision maker

Summary

Now that you have finished this book you should be able to:

- recognize when you do – and when you do not – have to take a decision
- distinguish between routine and non-routine decisions
- choose an appropriate method of decision making
- gather data from a variety of sources
- collect quality information
- assess data and information storage systems for accessibility and security
- use a variety of techniques to organize quantitative data
- take a rational decision
- comment on the use of other decision-making techniques
- minimize the risks associated with decision taking
- present information to decision makers
- guide people who are taking routine decisions
- inform other people of decisions effectively
- evaluate your effectiveness as a decision maker

Recommended reading

Checklist 012 Solving problems
Checklist 013 Carrying out an information audit
Checklist 015 Making rational decisions
Checklist 051 Report writing
Checklist 080 Designing questionnaires
The Institute of Management Foundation

Jay, Ros (1994) *How to Write Proposals and Reports that Get Results*, Pitman Publishing and The Institute of Management Foundation

Michelli, Dena and McWilliams, Fiona (1996) *Networking*, Management Directions, The Institute of Management Foundation

Michelli, Dena and Straw, Alison (1995) *Successful Networking in a Week*, Headway Hodder & Stoughton and The Institute of Management

Norton, Bob (1995) *Managing Information in a Week*, Headway Hodder & Stoughton and The Institute of Management Foundation

Peel, Malcolm (1995) *Successful Decision Making in a Week*, Headway Hodder & Stoughton and The Institute of Management Foundation

Rowntree, Derek (1991) *Statistics without Tears: a primer for non-mathematicians*, Penguin Books

Wilson, David A. (1996) *Managing Knowledge*, Butterworth-Heinemann and The Institute of Management Foundation

Wilson, David A. (1993) *Managing Information*, Butterworth-Heinemann and The Institute of Management Foundation

About the Institute of Management

The mission of the Institute of Management (IM) is to promote the development, exercise and recognition of professional management.

The IM is the leading professional organization for managers. Its efforts and resources are devoted to ensuring the continuing development and success of its members.

At the forefront of management standards, the IM provides a range of services for its members. These include flexible training programmes and a unique range of support services such as career counselling, enquiry and research facilities and preferential prices on IM publications and other IM products.

Further details about the Institute of Management may be obtained from:

Institute of Management
Management House
Cottingham Road
Corby
Northants
NN17 1TT

Telephone 01536 204222

We need your views

We really need your views in order to make the Institue of Management Open Learning Programme an even better learning tool for you. Please take time out to complete and return this questionnaire to Tessa Gingell, Pergamon Open Learning, Linacre House, Jordan Hill, Oxford OX2 8DP.

Name:..

Address:...

....

Title of workbook:...

If applicable, please state which qualification you are studying for. If not, please describe what study you are undertaking, and with which organization or college:

....

Please grade the following out of 10 (10 being extremely good, 0 being extremely poor):

Content: ....   Suitability for ability level: ....

Readability: ....   Qualification coverage: ....

What did you particularly like about this workbook?

....

Are there any features you disliked about this workbook? Please identify them.

....

Are there any errors we have missed?
If so, please state page number: ....

How are you using the material? For example, as an open learning course, as a reference resource, as a training resource, etc.

....

How did you hear about the Institue of Management Open Learning Programme?:

Word of mouth: Through my tutor/trainer: Mailshot:

Other (please give details):...

Many thanks for your help in returning this form.

Institute of Management Open Learning Programme

This programme comprises seventeen workbooks, each on a core management topic with the latest management thinking, as well as a *User Guide* and a *Mentor Guide*.

Designed for self study through open learning, the workbooks cover all management experience from team building to budgeting, from the skills of self management to manage strategically for organizational success.

TITLE	ISBN	Price
The Influential Manager	0 7506 3662 9	£22.50
Managing Yourself	0 7506 3661 0	£22.50
Getting the Right People to Do the Right Job	0 7506 3660 2	£22.50
Understanding Business Process Management	0 7506 3659 9	£22.50
Customer Focus	0 7506 3663 7	£22.50
Getting TQM to Work	0 7506 3664 5	£22.50
Leading from the Front	0 7506 3665 3	£22.50
Improving Your Organization's Success	0 7506 3666 1	£22.50
Project Management	0 7506 3667 X	£22.50
Budgeting and Financial Control	0 7506 3668 8	£22.50
Effective Financial and Resource Management	0 7506 3669 6	£22.50
Developing Yourself and Your Staff	0 7506 3670 X	£22.50
Building a High Performance Team	0 7506 3671 8	£22.50
The New Model Leader	0 7506 3672 6	£22.50
Making Rational Decisions	0 7506 3673 4	£22.50
Communication	0 7506 3674 2	£22.50
Successful Information Management	0 7506 3675 0	£22.50
User Guide	0 7506 3676 9	£22.50
Mentor Guide	0 7506 3677 7	£22.50
Full set of workbooks plus *Mentor Guide* and *User Guide*	0 7506 3359 X	£370.00

To order: *(Please quote ISBNs when ordering)*

- College Orders: 01865 314333
- Account holders: 01865 314301
- Individual Purchases: 01865 314627

(Please have credit card details ready)

For further information or to request a full series brochure, please contact:

Tessa Gingell on 01865 314477